T0319059

Cambridge Elements ≡

Elements in the Philosophy of Immanuel Kant
edited by
Desmond Hogan
Princeton University
Howard Williams
University of Cardiff
Allen Wood
Indiana University

THE GUARANTEE OF PERPETUAL PEACE

Wolfgang Ertl

Keio University, Tokyo

CAMBRIDGE
UNIVERSITY PRESS

CAMBRIDGE
UNIVERSITY PRESS

University Printing House, Cambridge CB2 8BS, United Kingdom

One Liberty Plaza, 20th Floor, New York, NY 10006, USA

477 Williamstown Road, Port Melbourne, VIC 3207, Australia

314–321, 3rd Floor, Plot 3, Splendor Forum, Jasola District Centre,
New Delhi – 110025, India

79 Anson Road, #06–04/06, Singapore 079906

Cambridge University Press is part of the University of Cambridge.

It furthers the University's mission by disseminating knowledge in the pursuit of
education, learning, and research at the highest international levels of excellence.

www.cambridge.org
Information on this title: www.cambridge.org/9781108438834
DOI: 10.1017/9781108529785

First published 2020

A catalogue record for this publication is available from the British Library.

ISBN 978-1-108-43883-4 Paperback
ISSN 2397-9461 (online)
ISSN 2514-3824 (print)

The Guarantee of Perpetual Peace

Elements in the Philosophy of Immanuel Kant

DOI: 10.1017/9781108529785
First published online: February 2020

Wolfgang Ertl
Keio University, Tokyo

Abstract: This Element addresses three questions about Kant's guarantee thesis by examining the "first addendum" of his *Philosophical Sketch*: how the guarantor powers interrelate, how there can be a guarantee without undermining freedom and why there is a guarantee in the first place. Kant's conception of an interplay of human and divine rational agency encompassing nature is crucial: on moral grounds, we are warranted to believe the "world author" knew that if he were to bring about the world, the "supreme" good would come about too. Perpetual peace is the condition that enables the supreme good to be realized in history.

Keywords: Kant, Immanuel, philosophy of history, theory of peace, postulates of pure practical reason, Molinism, history of

ISBNs: 9781108438834 (PB), 9781108529785 (OC)
ISSNS: 2397-9461 (online), 2514-3824 (print)

Contents

1 Introduction

In his book, *Perpetual Peace: A Philosophical Sketch*[1] (1795), Kant develops a normative account of politics based on the three pillars of state law, international law and cosmopolitan law which, together, when generally obeyed, he thinks sustain perpetual peace, the "highest political good" (MM 6: 355).

The precise nature of the institutional framework within which this is supposed to happen has been the topic of intense debate. At times, Kant seems to hold on to an ideal of a world republic (see TPP VIII, 8: 358, 379), which is basically a higher-order state consisting of particular states as its members. However, in other passages it seems as though he backtracks toward a mere, albeit constantly expanding federation of states (see TPP 8: 354, 357).[2]

Kant also presents a number of considerations, in the broadest of terms, on how to make perpetual peace a historical 'reality' while doing justice both to political craftsmanship and the demands of morality (TPP 8: 368–386). In fact, for Kant it is crucial to integrate political craftsmanship into a moral mindset of political agents.[3]

His suggestions amount to something like a gradualist or reformist approach, with an emphasis on not endangering the existing legal conditions in their as yet imperfect state, while improving them in the direction required by his normative legal considerations.

When Kant outlines the special role he reserves for philosophy in this process, he stresses that philosophers need to be granted a safe space for their investigations regarding peace (TPP 8: 368–369). In line, presumably with his mature account of public reason,[4] which focuses on the philosophical faculties at the universities as its institutional home, he regards philosophy as providing the intellectual resources required for political agency committed to perpetual peace.

On top of these normative considerations, however, Kant includes a surprising "addendum" (TPP 8: 360–368) and switches to what looks, on the face of it, like a descriptive statement about the certainty of the 'desired' as much as morally required outcome of perpetual peace.

---

[1] I suggest this translation of the original title *Zum ewigen Frieden: Ein philosophischer Entwurf* leaving the amalgamated form "zum" untranslated since, as far as I can see, the equivocation in German making the meaning oscillate between "toward," "on" and "(dedicated) to" cannot be preserved in English. Perhaps the most widely known rendering of the title is Mary J. Gregor's *Toward Perpetual Peace: A Philosophical Project* in Kant (1996b), 311–351. A list of abbreviations can be found at the end of this Element.

[2] See Höffe (2004), Kleingeld (2004) and Pogge (2009) among many others. The correct reading of the passage in TPP 8: 357 is, however, highly contentious.

[3] For an account of Kant's theory of politics, see, for example, Gerhardt (1999).

[4] As laid out in CF of 1798. See Ertl (2017a) for details.

The section is puzzling in many respects: It abounds with material seemingly pertaining to the kind of epistemologically overambitious metaphysics that was to be overcome through a critique of pure reason. Understanding the peculiar status of this material, however, is crucial since it provides the clue to the following important questions that arise in connection with the guarantee thesis, namely: (i) What is the relation between the various powers Kant names as guarantors of perpetual peace and in particular providence and nature?; (ii) How is the presence of these guarantor powers compatible with human freedom?; (iii) Why is there a guarantee of perpetual peace in the first place?

As I am trying to show, the material under consideration belongs to what we can call "Kant's practically grounded metaphysics", that is, a set of doctrines about objects that transcend the bounds of sense. According to Kant, we are warranted in subscribing to these doctrines by virtue of his moral philosophy, without having the tools required to vindicate these claims from the point of view of theoretical knowledge.

To be sure, while the guarantee claim is not something belonging to theory, as Kant emphasizes (TPP 8: 362), even from the point of view of practical reason his move generates a number of problems, especially with regard to the double-faced character of perpetual peace as an allegedly certain outcome of world history and as something we have the duty to work towards.

In this Element, I shall focus on this 'guarantee addendum', as I shall call it, in order to better understand Kant's seemingly contradictory claims and to show how they can be rendered coherent. Of particular interest will be the almost two Academy pages long first footnote of this section (TPP 8: 361.5–362.39)[5], the 'guarantee footnote', a much neglected and sometimes even maligned piece of text. As I shall argue, this footnote is not at all a foreign body in a treatise essentially concerned with political, legal and historical topics.

Rather, it is instrumental for outlining at least parts of Kant's practically grounded metaphysics on the basis of which his normative and descriptive claims can be shown to fit together.[6] As we shall see, this metaphysics involves but is by no means restricted to doctrines based on Kant's first postulate of pure practical reason.[7] Instead of dismissing these passages, the way forward

---

[5] To facilitate referencing, I have added the line numbers of the Academy edition pagination wherever convenient and helpful.

[6] "Metaphysics," however, does not by itself refer to a discipline concerned with transcendent objects in Kant. For a recent discussion of alternative notions of metaphysics, including a metaphysical reading of transcendental idealism, and their importance for Kant's political philosophy, focusing on its normative dimension, see Baiasu, Pihlström and Williams (2011).

[7] This doctrine is of course highly controversial in its own right. In large part, the pertinent debates boil down to a fundamental disagreement with regard to what is nowadays called the ethics of belief. While evidentialists deny that it can ever be rational to believe something without evidence, pragmatists endorse this claim. Kant's position is clearly close to that of the pragmatists

suggested in this Element is, therefore, to further explore the territory Kant is treading upon there by drawing on similar and related texts in Kant's œuvre.

Throughout the guarantee addendum Kant clearly – and presumably to the irritation of many a contemporary reader – does assume the existence of God and his "end" as a "world author" (TPP 8: 361.7–8fn), emphasizing at the same time that such an assumption is feasible only on practical grounds. As is well known, Kant has provided what he often calls a "moral" argument or even "proof" for the existence claim in all the three *Critiques*,[8] while the stress on an end on the part of God suggests that his version of it in the final paragraphs of the *Critique of the Power of Judgement* (i.e., §§84–91) – a highly prominent place in his œuvre since along with them the entire critical enterprise comes to its overall conclusion (see CJ 5: 170) – is particularly pertinent here.[9]

The common feature of Kant's different versions of the moral argument is that the autonomy-based categorical demands of duty, in consonance with our justified, ineliminable but at the same time secondary quest for happiness, require the assumption of a God conceived in terms of classic theist predicates such as omniscience and omnipotence. However, the striking feature of the version in the third *Critique* is that here Kant intricately interweaves the divine and the human perspective with regard to an overall aim of rational agency. Put briefly, while from our perspective the possibility of a necessary connection of happiness in proportion to morality is what matters, from the (human conception of the) divine point of view the success of the creative enterprise as a whole hinges on at least some human rational agents developing a good will. There is therefore a sense in which the bringing about of an end of creation can, from a practical point

---

in this domain. See Willaschek (2016) for a thoroughgoing discussion of these issues. Since the aim of this Element is mainly to understand Kant's argument about perpetual peace rather than to defend it, I will not enter this discussion any further. Long before this debate, Yovel (1980: 100, 109, 272), arguing mainly from a Hegelian perspective, simply dismissed Kant's reliance on this postulate as a *"deus ex machina"*-strategy leading to tensions within the critical system itself.

[8] CPR A809/B837–A819/B847; CPrR 5: 124–132; CJ 5: 447–453. See also PhilTh-P 28: 1010–1012 and 1081–1091. I am, of course, not suggesting that the political agents endorse, or need to endorse, the postulates in order to enter the realm of politics.

[9] Karl Ameriks (2012: 251) has recently stressed the overall importance of the closing passages of CJ for the whole critical project, insofar as Kant provides the idea of a "guarantee" – and Ameriks is using this very term here, "that our actions somehow do get the necessarily right consequences" as far as the highest good is concerned. I am drawing on Ameriks' insight here and in the remainder of this Element. In Ameriks (2012) – building on earlier approaches by Cassirer and Velkley and expanding on Ameriks (2006) – he has outlined the significance in Kant of a teleological account of history that converges toward the highest good. Ameriks takes this account to be integrated in Kant's purposive interpretation of the actuality of the world altogether. In the following, I shall try to apply this idea to the issue of perpetual peace and go beyond Ameriks' own approach in two respects: (a) I will focus on perpetual peace as a condition for the highest good; and (b) I shall consider the specifics of the divine perspective given the reading of the theist predicates Kant endorses and, in this respect, also go beyond what Kant himself discusses explicitly.

of view, be said to have been 'handed over' or delegated to human agents to achieve.[10]

The text of this Element is structured as follows: After this very brief account of the background and contents of the essay *Perpetual Peace*, I shall discuss in detail key passages of the guarantee addendum and the guarantee footnote almost in its entirety. A considerable amount of attention will be focused on a somewhat arcane sentence in the guarantee footnote, according to which the form of the sensual world underlying its existence can only be rendered comprehensible or intelligible by referring to the end of the "world author" that determines this form beforehand (TPP 8: 361.5–8fn). Taking "beforehand" to mean at least "logically prior to its existence" and drawing on both an epistemic and a constitutive meaning of "determining," what turns out be at issue here is a grand scale vision of God's thoughts 'before' the creation of the world – an idea that is sometimes inaccurately attributed to Hegel, but is rather part and parcel of scholastic treatises on God.

The main problem with this reading is that – even from a practical perspective – it seems to shift agency away from the human to the divine subject contemplating which laws of nature to enact in order to realize the divine plan. While this idea explains – answering question (i) from the list above – how nature and providence can coincide with regard to the function of guaranteeing perpetual peace, it raises the problem of human freedom since our freedom is required in view of the duty to work for the realization of perpetual peace in the first place.

Therefore, various different aspects or facets of the problem of freedom, all pertinent to the topic at issue, will be discussed in section 3; in order to do this we have to draw on textual material from outside the essay *Perpetual Peace*, since in this text Kant considers these issues to be settled. As we shall see, potential threats for human freedom arise not only from within his practically grounded metaphysics, but – perhaps even more prominently – from doctrines belonging to Kant's theoretical philosophy, such as the natural causal

---

[10] This idea has been emphasized by Yovel (1980: 79), for whom "[t]he final end of the world is not inherent in it *per se*, as in a thing in itself," but "projected on it by man's moral consciousness and . . . realized by his praxis in history". While I also agree with Yovel that, in Kant, God is at the service of man rather than the other way round (Yovel 1980: 116), and that it is the primary function of God to provide the potential for the actualization of the highest good, in my opinion the idea of a guarantee of perpetual peace is essentially related to the actualization of the unconditional element of the highest good and to the issue of bridging the gulf between practical reason and nature in this respect. This bridging, as we shall see in section 3, is rather the task of Kant's peculiar form of compatibilism on the basis of transcendental idealism. Moreover, according to Kant's conception of God, provided by the postulate, God must be assumed to have a special kind of knowledge about the actualization of the highest good through human agency.

determinism underlying the mechanism of nature. In any case, Kant's commitment to freedom as required by morality constitutes a further thread in his practically grounded metaphysics, and the same is true for the arguments establishing the unity of practical and theoretical reason. Kant's position with regard to the natural causal facet of the problem of freedom – answering question (ii) – will be shown to be a focal point for all the other facets and to amount to an unconventional version of compatibilism according to which the contents of at least some laws of nature depend on human freedom.

Finally, in section 4, I will turn to a discussion of the highest good and the place of perpetual peace in it, in particular the sometimes so-called "secular" or world immanent variant of the highest good within the framework of the ethical commonwealth, as explored in the third piece of *Religion within the Boundaries of Mere Reason*. Perpetual peace, or to be more precise, an imperfect variant of perpetual peace, is shown to be indispensable for the ethical commonwealth as a condition of its possibility. The ethical commonwealth, in turn, is the social context within which the free acquisition of a good will can occur.

Although he himself nowhere explicitly connects these considerations to the question at issue, Kant reads the pertinent and appropriately qualified theist predicates of omniscience and omnipotence in a way which allows us to assume on practical grounds that God has the capacity to bring about the world on the basis of his knowledge about and his ability to provide conditions (through the mechanism of nature) under which at least some human agents would, by their very freedom, turn the world into a success. It is this move which allows us, again on the basis of ultimately practical considerations, to infer assumptions about the successful outcome of the creative enterprise through human agency. The claim of perpetual peace and its certainty to come about needs to be understood in the context of these ideas insofar as it is both an intermediary end from the divine perspective and an intermediary duty that needs to be met from the human perspective, a combination which – from a practical standpoint and answering question (iii) – establishes the certainty of its achievement. As the highest political good, it is the condition required to hold for the overall success of rational agency to materialize in history by making the ethical commonwealth possible.

In the concluding remarks, I shall argue that emphasizing the importance of Kant's practically grounded metaphysics does not undermine the normative foundations of human agency. With the preservation of freedom, both the grounding of moral obligations in autonomy and the importance or even the predicament of having to make the right decisions on the part of the political agents remain fully intact. The human need for deliberations and appropriate decisions is not eliminated by concerns about predicting how we will ultimately bring about perpetual peace. We need rather to stick to the preliminary and definitive articles and our morally informed political skills in putting them into practice. In all this, the real possibility of perpetual peace is taken as given through there being the duty to bring it about in the first place.

2 The Guarantee Addendum

In this section, after a brief look at the epistemological status of the doctrines under examination, a rather detailed account of important paragraphs of the guarantee addendum will be provided, focusing on the relation between the various guarantor powers Kant names in these passages. Next, the various types of interplay between different kinds of causes involved in processes integral to the achievement of perpetual peace, discussed by Kant in the guarantor footnote, will be investigated. This includes Kant's distinction of many-sided forms of *concursus* and providence, a proper understanding of which is required for clarifying the relation of providence to nature. Finally, I will examine how these passages relate to other texts by Kant and will offer something like a brief contextual reading of this section of the *Perpetual Peace* essay.

2.1 Preliminaries

One of the most striking and, for some readers at least, perhaps even disconcerting features of the guarantee addendum and, in particular, the guarantee footnote (TPP 8: 361.5–362.39), is the presence and indeed prevalence of concepts prominent in scholastic (especially early modern scholastic) philosophy, such as "providence" and *concursus* relating to God's causal role with regard to events in space and time. Moreover, and as we shall see in detail below, Kant clearly commits himself to finely tuned positions that endorse such a role. This seems to fly in the face of the results of his project of a critique of pure reason, one of which is that knowledge of objects is restricted to the realm on this side of the bounds of sense. While it is contentious as to whether Kant's transcendental idealism is itself a form of metaphysics, it is clear that he denies the possibility of knowledge of objects beyond the bounds of sense, that is, the feasibility of transcendent metaphysics as a theoretical science. However, this does not preclude the pertinent claims he makes in the guarantee addendum from having a different function.

Kant takes the existence of God as well as God's objective ultimate end as given throughout these passages and this can give us a decisive hint. In Kant's œuvre, it is the task of the so-called moral argument[11] to back up these claims, and

---

[11] See Footnote 9 above. Baiasu (2018: 184–7), mostly with regard to Taylor (2010), discusses the role of the first postulate with regard to the guarantee issue, but focuses on the possibility of

there is no indication that he is departing from or revoking this strategy here. In addition to this, the moral argument is supposed to be able to give us a determinate concept of God. In the relevant passages of the *Critiques,* Kant only mentions the traditional theist predicates contained in this concept, but the apparently foreign and unfitting considerations in the guarantee addendum can best be regarded as going into much more detail for the purpose of conceptual clarification. The question then is: What should we make of the very theses about, for example, God's role with regard to events in space and time? In the light of what has been said about the moral argument, one plausible suggestion is to treat these theses as corollaries of taking God – on practical grounds – to be a perfect rational *agent* equipped with traditional theist properties, while at the same time upholding the results established in Kant's transcendental philosophy – for example, the validity of the principles of the understanding, such as the second analogy of experience, and the methodological naturalism that comes along with them. We shall see how far we can get with this idea in the discussion of the guarantee addendum.

In the literature, the term "practico-dogmatic metaphysics"[12] has been suggested to cover the set of such claims about transcendent objects – for example, in our case, the perplexing thesis that we may consider God to be the sufficient cause of natural events in the world (TPP 8: 362. 26–28fn). Since "dogmatic" has the air of the illegitimate (although Kant himself sometimes uses this term in a much more neutral sense, and this even in TPP 8: 362.10), one might wish to consider using "practico-transcendent metaphysics" or "practically grounded metaphysics" instead. The term "practical" is in any case more suitable than "moral" in order to distinguish this set of claims from Kant's metaphysics of morals which is concerned with normative issues.

In the following, I will use the phrase "practically grounded metaphysics" in order to emphasize its peculiar epistemic status. As we shall see in section 3, Kant's investigations about transcendental freedom (which, according to him, we are committed to by virtue of the categorical imperative) can plausibly also be read as belonging to such a practically grounded metaphysics. The same is true for at least some of his doctrines regarding the compatibility of transcendental

---

perpetual peace. Ultimately, in line with Taylor (2010: 13), Baiasu rejects the idea of this postulate being pertinent here. In my approach, the first postulate is indeed pertinent, for the certain future actuality, not the possibility of perpetual peace, although only in a rather indirect manner, by accounting for the certain future actuality of the supreme good of virtue or moral self-perfection. The certain future actuality of moral self-perfection follows from features of the concept of God generated by the argument for this postulate.

[12] See Zöller (2016) for a detailed discussion of these issues. As far as the label in question is concerned, Zöller, who favors "practico-dogmatic metaphysics," can admittedly draw on Kant's own usage of the term "praktisch-dogmatisch" (XX, 311) in connection with metaphysics here. Mertens (1995: 240) simply speaks of "praktische() Metaphysik."

freedom and natural causal determinism. Hence, "practically grounded metaphysics" – in my opinion – has at least what we can call a theist, a libertarian and something like a compatibilist dimension, thereby ensuring that the first two dimensions are both mutually coherent and coherent with the results of Kant's theoretical philosophy, in particular the transcendental account of experience. As I shall point out, part of the difficulty with understanding the guarantee addendum is due to the fact that in these passages Kant is only dealing with the theist segment of this type of metaphysics and its coherence with the transcendental approach. For the other dimensions we need to draw on different material in Kant's œuvre.

2.2 The Guarantor Powers

We can now turn to the text of the guarantee addendum. This section (TPP 8: 360.10–368.20) is divided into the main text consisting of eight unnumbered paragraphs and four footnotes, the first of which extends over no less than five pages in the second, pertinent edition of *Perpetual Peace* and deserves our particular attention, although, of course, not just for this reason. The main text starts off with an introductory paragraph elucidating the relationship between nature, fate and providence and their role as the guarantor of perpetual peace. It is here that Kant also recommends focusing on nature when it comes to theory as opposed to religion, and it is fair to say that the main treatment of providence is delegated (which by no means suggests "relegated") to the huge footnote. The key passage[13] in this first paragraph of the main text, cast in a sentence of stunning syntactic complexity even according to the demanding standards of Kant's notoriously hypotactic prose, reads as below. I shall start with the German original and then try to provide a translation that is as literal as possible.

> Das, was diese *Gewähr* (Garantie) leistet, ist nichts Geringeres als die große Künstlerin, *Natur* (*natura daedala rerum*), aus deren mechanischem Laufe sichtbarlich Zweckmäßigkeit hervorleuchtet, durch die Zwietracht der Menschen Eintracht selbst wider ihren Willen emporkommen zu lassen, und darum, gleich als Nöthigung einer ihren Wirkungsgesetzen nach uns unbekannten Ursache, *Schicksal*, bey Erwägung aber ihrer Zweckmäßigkeit im Laufe der Welt, als tief liegende Weisheit einer höheren, auf den objektiven Endzweck des menschlichen Geschlechts gerichteten, und diesen Weltlauf prädeterminirenden Ursache, *Vorsehung* genannt wird, die wir zwar *eigentlich* nicht an diesen Kunstanstalten der Natur *erkennen*, oder auch nur daraus auf sie *schliessen*, sondern (wie in aller Beziehung der Form der Dinge auf Zwecke überhaupt) nur *hinzudenken* können und müssen, um uns von ihrer Möglichkeit, nach der

---

[13] For a first attempt at dissecting this sentence, mainly with regard to the relation of the guarantor powers, see Ertl (2018).

Analogie menschlicher Kunsthandlungen, einen Begriff zu machen, deren Verhältniß und Zusammenstimmung aber zu dem Zwecke, den uns die Vernunft unmittelbar vorschreibt (dem moralischen), sich vorzustellen, eine Idee ist, die zwar in *theoretischer* Hinsicht überschwenglich, in *praktischer* aber (z.B. in Ansehung des Pflichtbegriffs *vom ewigen Frieden*, um jenen Mechanism der Natur dazu zu benutzen) dogmatisch und ihrer Realität nach wohl gegründet ist.[14]

The translation is as follows:

That which provides this liability (guarantee) is nothing less than the great artist nature (*natura daedala rerum*) in whose mechanical course purposiveness visibly shines forth, to let unity come up through the disunity of men even against their will, and [which] is therefore called fate like a compulsion through a cause unbeknownst to us with regard to its laws of efficacy, and when considering its purposefulness in the course of the world, as a deeplying wisdom of a higher cause directed to the objective ultimate end of the human species and predetermining this course of the world, called providence, which strictly speaking we do not know from these institutions of art in nature and cannot even infer from them but (as in all relations of the form of things to ends as such) we can and must add in thinking, in order to have a concept of its possibility in analogy to human actions of art, but to imagine the relation of it and consonance to the end (the moral one) immediately prescribed by reason is an idea which is effusive in a theoretical respect, but which in a practical respect (for example, with regard to the concept of the duty of perpetual peace, in order to use that mechanism of nature for it) is dogmatic and well grounded concerning its reality. (TPP 8: 360.12–362.11, my translation)

Strikingly, Kant calls the guarantor power "nature",[15] but at the same time provides two alternative labels for it, namely "fate"[16] and "providence".[17] Moreover, there are two possible ways of reading the syntax of the sentence

---

[14] German quotations from TPP are from the second, expanded original edition, that is, Kant (1796), retaining Kant's punctuation and spelling which is slightly different both from contemporary German and the Academy version.

[15] See, for example, Förster (2009) and Deligiorgi (2006) for a comprehensive account of nature as the guarantor power, albeit mainly with regard to IUH.

[16] The perhaps surprising inclusion of "fate" here is probably echoing M §975 in which Baumgarten speaks of *"fortuna,"* even *"fortuna() sancta()"* in connection with providence, although Baumgarten himself uses "Glück" as the German equivalent. I shall try to indicate later how Kant's Molinist intuitions can, in some measure, also explain the inclusion of fate as a tag for the guarantor power.

[17] Lehner (2007) has provided a detailed examination of Kant's doctrine of providence throughout his œuvre, mainly with regard to his sources in German school philosophy and theology, while Lloyd (2009) attempted something like a rational reconstruction of providence in terms of progress. Frierson (2007) raises, among many other points, the important question regarding the extent to which providence needs to become part of Kant's doctrine of religion, which is, in turn, crucial for the ethical commonwealth.

quoted above. On the first reading, the relative clause beginning in the second line of the quotation (i.e., "aus deren ... " ["in whose ... "]) is elliptical with Kant leaving out a relative pronoun "die" ("which") in the fourth line before "darum" ("therefore"). This pronoun, had it been there, would have to refer to "Natur" ("nature"). On the second reading, the relative clause starting immediately after the demonstrative pronoun "das" ("that") at the very beginning of the quotation is "was ... leistet ... und ... genannt wird" ("which provides ... and is called"), thus the overall subclause is not elliptical after all. In this case, the absence of a relative pronoun in the fourth line would indicate that the reference is still to "das" ("that") in the first line. I take the second reading to be the correct one, but whether the first or second reading is correct does not really affect my interpretation, although the second perhaps fits it better.

In line with the second reading, Kant is saying that the guarantor is called "fate" ("Schicksal") insofar as the device of producing unity through strife is taken as necessitation or coercion through an *unknown* cause. Note, though, that the personification of nature as the great artist occurs prior to the identification of the guarantor as fate. Moreover, in a further step of reflection the guarantor is taken to be "providence" ("Vorsehung"), and this connects it to a wise cause that aims at the objective ultimate purpose of humanity.[18] It is this move in particular which has been met with surprise, to say the least. Providence, for Kant, is accounted for with regard to purposiveness (in terms of an analogy to the production of artefacts). At the same time, he considers the idea of providence being in agreement with this ultimate purpose, that is, presumably as instrumental for its fulfillment, to be "effusive" ("überschwenglich") in theoretical terms, but feasible in practical contexts. As an example of such a practical context, Kant proposes "to use that mechanism of nature for it," and "it" in all likelihood refers to the "concept of duty of perpetual peace."

Kant obviously does not regard the workings of the mechanism of nature, nor that of providence,[19] as incompatible with freedom as a requirement of duty,

---

[18] For an overview of different opinions in the literature as to how nature and providence are related see Hoesch (2014: 319–327). I agree with Kleingeld (2001: 219) that, by and large, Kant uses the term "nature" in order to emphasize "that historical progress is supported by natural means" and that " '(p)rovidence' is the more apt term for stressing that this order of nature must be regarded as caused by a highest wisdom." Moreover, according to Kleingeld, Kant intends to emphasize through the usage of the term "(p)rovidence" that the moral subject needs to "postulate the existence of a moral author of the world as the precondition of the realizability of moral ends in the world" (Kleingeld (2001: 219). In fact, I am trying to examine Kant's metaphysical commitments that underpin this idea, in particular with regard to a very special moral end, the establishment of an ethical commonwealth.

[19] See Bouton (2007) for the important observation that, contrary to what one might think, providence is not necessarily incompatible with human freedom, at least with regard to certain conceptions of it. As I will try to point out below, Kant's conception of providence is in precisely

and he emphasizes the character of perpetual peace as a concept of duty. Later in the text he suggests that perpetual peace is closely connected to the final objective end prescribed by reason (TPP 8: 365.21–3).

I shall postpone a discussion of the compatibility problem(s) with regard to human freedom that arise here, and turn instead to the perplexing plethora of, on the face of it, different ends that Kant talks about in the opening passage of the guarantee addendum.

These are: (a) the objective ultimate end of a higher wisdom, that is, in all likelihood, God; (b) "the" end immediately prescribed by reason as a duty; and (c) perpetual peace as a duty or as covered by a concept of duty. Kant moves with striking ease from what looks like theological considerations in (a) to considerations pertaining to moral duties in (b) and (c), which, to be sure, do not apply in the case of God and his perfect will.

Let us start by looking at the connection between (b) and (c): As far as the relationship of perpetual peace to the end immediately prescribed by reason is concerned, suffice it to say here that the phrase "the end" could in principle be just a placeholder for "any end (immediately prescribed by reason)." In this case, perpetual peace would just be one of these ends. While this reading is a theoretical possibility, it is not very likely since one would expect an indefinite article instead, that is, something like "an end immediately prescribed by reason."

If "the end" in question is different from perpetual peace, what could it be? Since Kant is concerned here with ends to be brought about rather than preexisting ends, it is, most probably, an end which is at the same time a duty, one of the key topics of the *Doctrine of Virtue*; there are two main candidates for such an end, namely, self-perfection and the happiness of others (MM 6: 385sq.). The adjective "immediately" would suggest something related to the agent personally and not to a third person, hence self-perfection looks like the more plausible option. "Immediately" may even rule out the nonmoral dimension of self-perfection (see MM 6: 392), since experience is required to find out which talents one possesses and, therefore, are supposed to be cultivated. Hence "the end" should be moralization or the full development of moral capacities.

On the other hand, physical self-cultivation is the ultimate end of nature, albeit only an intermediary end of creation as such in the CJ (5: 429–434)[20], and

---

this regard similar to Luis de Molina's. See Flint (1998) for a detailed account of the Molinist version of providence.

[20] It is in this passage (see particularly CJ 5: 430) that Kant even concedes that war can have a function in bringing about a legal condition of the relationship between states and thus also for the physical cultivation of the agents. This, to be sure, is evidently not a justification of war, but an attempt to show that even morally wrong action can provide a positive contribution to the overall scheme of creation and the duties to be fulfilled therein by the creaturely agents.

for this end a "cosmopolitan whole" which, we can safely add, sustains perpetual peace, is the proximate means, so to speak. Since physical self-cultivation is also an end and at the same time a duty, one could argue that it is precisely the one referred to in (b) above. Clearly, though, moral self-cultivation has priority in Kant, with physical self-cultivation, in turn, being a precondition for the success of moral self-cultivation in terms of the acquisition of a stable good will. Kant's usage of the definite article in the passage from the *Perpetual Peace* essay under consideration (8: 361.7) suggests that he indeed has in mind one end which is at the same time a duty and, since he uses the term "moral" to characterize this end, I take this to be moral self-perfection.

The next question, of course, is moralization of whom? Kant is talking about the human species, or humankind, in connection with the end in question. This phrase leaves it open as to precisely who is the subject of this moralization, since it is only individual agents who can achieve it. Kant's phrase is not only compatible with a universal and a particular reading, that is, the moralization of each and every human being or of just a limited number, but the possible grammatical function of "des menschlichen Geschlechts" ("of the human species") as a *genitivus subiectivus* manages to establish a vital connection to the objective ultimate end of a higher wisdom. Taken this way, the phrase does not indicate an end humankind ought to have but states that the human species or humankind itself *is* God's end. This gives us a first hint at the connection between (a) and (b): The objective ultimate end of God is – or at least is essentially concerned with – the moralization of all, or at least some, human agents, provided we can understand "human species" in an emphatic sense, involving the actualization of the moral capacities of all or at least some of its members. We shall see in a moment, when looking at the guarantee footnote, that such a reading is indeed plausible.

The idea of taking at least some divine ends as the fulfillment of human duties will be crucial for approaching the idea of a guarantee of perpetual peace. The hitch, of course, is that in a Kantian environment, human agents need to bring about their moral perfection essentially by themselves.

Since (b) and (c) are different in the reading suggested, what is the relation between these two? Again, the details of this question will be discussed below. One way of reading Kant here is that he is assuming something like a hierarchy of both divine ends and human duties, in which some divine ends which are at the same time human duties are subordinate to others. Consequently, what is in one sense an end can at the same time be a means to something else. In a similar vein, the successful fulfillment of one duty may be a condition for the fulfillment of another. As I will argue in section 4 below, this structure is pertinent for understanding Kant with regard to the duty to work towards perpetual peace. Seen this way, the successful compliance with the duty of (working towards) perpetual peace is indeed a precondition for the successful fulfillment of a different, very special moral duty in the Kantian system, namely, the duty addressed to mankind of establishing the ethical commonwealth (see Rel 6: 94).

A further difficult question is whether perpetual peace is meant to precede or to come along together with ethical cultivation, and it seems that, at least in *Perpetual Peace*, moralization occurs within the safety of perpetual peace (TPP 8: 366). This will turn out to be consistent with the distinction between an imperfect and a perfect variant of perpetual peace.

Paradoxically, Kant's remark about God's end evokes a notion of divine agency as being involved, if not dominant, here, and this leads to a further issue. What I have in mind is Kant's phrase "to use that mechanism of nature for it." The obvious question that arises with regard to this idea, just as in the case of moralization, is that concerning the subject of such "usage." Does it refer to the intellectual enterprise carried out in this section as a whole insofar as we (along, of course, with mainly Kant himself), who are reflecting on the feasibility of perpetual peace, may "use" – in the sense of "draw on" – the notion of a mechanism of nature to come to terms with this problem? This reading may be called the "reflective usage reading." Or does it refer to something more mundane like deliberation, in particular political deliberation, in that human agents, especially those in charge of political entities, are supposed to *utilize* the mechanism of nature in order to achieve the ends to which they are obligated by practical reason? This interpretation may be called the "technical usage reading." I will try to show below that neither reading, nor their combination, is fully plausible, or at least that neither can capture all that Kant has in mind here.

2.3 The Guarantee Thesis

With this in mind, we can now turn to Kant's guarantee thesis. At the end of the guarantee addendum Kant says:

> In this manner nature guarantees perpetual peace through the mechanism in human inclinations itself; with a certainty to be sure, which is not sufficient to (theoretically) prophesy the future of it, but which is enough in a practical respect, and makes it a duty to work towards this (not only chimerical) end. (TPP 8: 368.15–20, my translation)

I take the term "certainty" ("Sicherheit") here not to indicate a psychological property of a judgment or claim, but that we are warranted in maintaining the proposition in question. In this manner, it may indeed be something like an epistemic property. In the case at issue, we are not warranted in a theoretical context to claim that perpetual peace will come about. But, what are we allowed to claim in this respect from a practical perspective?

At first view, this might seem to be a comparatively modest thesis, in that the contrast between a theoretical and practical perspective seems to coincide with claims concerning the future *actuality* and the mere (albeit real) *possibility* of perpetual peace respectively. In this vein, the guarantee of perpetual peace would both be a matter of the practical perspective and concern only its real possibility. One might think that this is only fitting because, for it to be a duty to work towards the establishment of perpetual peace, what we need is indeed the (real) possibility of perpetual peace, and this by virtue mainly of the principle "ought implies can." To be sure, in this sense, (real) possibility is only a necessary condition for this duty to hold, but still, establishing this possibility would be a substantial point. Kant's claim from the quotation above (TPP 8: 362.11) about the (presumably *objective*) "reality" of providence and its relation to and consonance with the end immediately prescribed by reason (even if this is not identical with perpetual peace) also, first and foremost, concerns its real possibility, not its actuality. Finally, the contrast Kant is making with "chimerical" may also be thought to indicate that perpetual peace is not impossible, which again would not necessarily amount to claiming its future actuality.

Still, there are indications that Kant understands the guarantee thesis in a more ambitious manner. Given the tenor of the overall text – for example, in the last sentence of the passage preceding the guarantee addendum (TPP 8: 360.7–9) – Kant does in fact have the prognosis of the future *actuality* of perpetual peace in mind, even though he concedes that such a claim falls short of genuine knowledge.

A distinction between a weak and a strong reading of the guarantee thesis has been suggested,[21] but both readings have been taken to be theoretical claims. According to the strong reading, "we can know that a state of affairs (perpetual peace) will take place" (Caranti 2012: 148). According to the weak reading, "we know (or [...] there are grounds to be confident) that we are constantly approximating that desired goal" (Caranti 2012: 148). In both cases, it is

---

[21] See Caranti (2012). In this paper, Caranti, taking on mainly Guyer's (2006) rather critical stance, discusses the key difficulties the guarantee thesis generates within Kant's philosophy and distinguishes between (i) an epistemic, (ii) an anthropological and (iii) a moral concern. With respect to (i), the problem is that even if we concede that the guarantee thesis is compatible with the strictures of Kant's critical program, there seems to be no theoretical or empirical reason to assume that history will converge towards perpetual peace. According to (ii), Kant's doctrine of radical evil casts doubt on the feasibility of a plan of nature to bring about perpetual peace. As far as (iii) is concerned, the presence of a guarantor power seems to undermine the duty to work towards perpetual peace. In this Element, I hope to be able to address all these concerns and to show that Kant can dispel them.

recommended that we abstract from the question what, after all, is the guarantor power.

It seems to me that these two versions each have a practically justified correlate in which knowledge or theoretical cognition is replaced by something like practically warranted or "moral belief", as Kant puts it in CPR A828/B856. Kant's overall emphasis on the practical mode renders these correlates more attractive, since they allow us to do justice both to the accentuation of the practical mode *and* the claim of the future actuality of perpetual peace.[22]

Which of the two practically justified correlates does Kant have in mind? One important point to consider is the notorious passage MM 6: 350, which appears to suggest that perpetual peace is not realiter possible after all. Does this thesis rule out the practical correlate of the strong reading? In any event, the MM passage is concerned with the object of the guarantee, not the guarantor; it is not any guarantor's fault that what is not realiter possible cannot be guaranteed in the sense of the state of affairs in question becoming actual at some point in time. Moreover, a denial of the real possibility of perpetual peace would of course rule out a fortiori even a reading of the guarantee thesis which takes it to secure precisely this real possibility. Conversely, there could plausibly only be a duty to "strive toward the constitutional perfection of one single state of nations" (Byrd and Hruschka 2010: 203).[23]

There is no indication at all that Kant denies the real possibility of perpetual peace in the essay *Perpetual Peace*; he rather seems to think that since there is the duty to bring it about, perpetual peace is realiter possible.[24] For this reason, I am going to ignore the MM passage here and focus on his position in the essay. Moreover, I will try to show that Kant does have the resources to establish the practical correlate of the strong reading, and I take this to cover the practical version of the weak variant as well. Due to space limitations, I will say little about Kant's idea of a mere asymptotic approach to perpetual peace (e.g., TPP

---

[22] Baiasu (2018: 193–197) is to be credited for drawing on Kant's doctrine of belief in order to elucidate the guarantee thesis, but he favors "doctrinal belief," that is, a form of assent still belonging to theory but, of course, short of knowledge. Baiasu (2018) also stresses that the doctrinal belief first and foremost concerns nature as the guarantor power but, on p. 197, at least comes close to shifting the justification of the guarantee thesis to "moral purposes" which is what I will be trying to argue for in detail in section 4.

[23] In any event, a full account of MM 6: 350 would require a consideration of the institutional setting of perpetual peace.

[24] Due to space limitations, I must omit a discussion of attempts to read Kant as employing or utilizing the guarantee thesis for political purposes, that is, in order to get political agents to work for the actualization of perpetual peace. See Flikschuh (2006) and Wood (2006: 257f) for this important topic. My focus on a practical variant of what Flikschuh (2006: 384) calls the "philosophy of history-reading," associated mainly with Yovel (1980) and contrasted with what she calls the "prudential reading," is by no means intended to downplay the significance of this topic.

8: 386). I take this to be indicative of his concession that he is indeed in a defensive position with regard to the future actuality reading of the guarantee claim. The mathematical notion of a limit indicates the outermost tip of actuality, as we can perhaps put it.[25]

In this vein, and as far as terminology is concerned, the term "future actuality reading" comprises both the weak and the strong version and is neutral as to whether this is intended to be a theoretically or a practically justified claim. The term "modest reading" covers anything short of the future actuality claim.[26]

2.4 Varieties of Cooperation

At any rate, we can expect to receive some elucidation of at least some of the points raised in the first paragraph of the guarantee addendum in the footnote referring to it (TPP 8: 361.5fn–362.39fn), although it must be said that it is a rather densely argued piece of writing, which does not immediately reveal its secrets. As we shall see, the guarantee footnote does indeed clarify important metaphysical issues related to providence and *concursus*. However, at least on the face of it, it also seems to put even more pressure on the idea that working toward perpetual peace on the part of humans is a matter of their freedom. Let us proceed step by step. Kant argues as follows:

> In the mechanism of nature to which the human being also belongs (as a sense entity) a form manifests itself which already lies at the ground of its existence and which we cannot render comprehensible other than by putting the end of a world author underneath it who determines it beforehand . . . (TPP 8: 361.5–8fn, my translation)

Kant's claim that as a "sense entity" ("Sinnenwesen") man, along with other entities, also belongs to nature alludes to his distinction between appearance and thing in itself, with sense entity corresponding, by and large, to appearance, with all the intricacies this distinction involves. One particularly important problem that arises here is due to the fact that Kant, throughout his writings, invokes two very different accounts of this distinction, namely, a so-called two-aspect (TA) and a so-called two-world (TW) model. It is not easy to pin down precisely what the difference is between these two models, particularly because a huge variety of different versions of each of them have been developed by Kant's commentators

---

[25] Caranti (2012: 160f.) himself wishes to uphold an even weaker version of the future actuality reading, but is adamant that this is a theoretical and empirical claim, indicating something like an objective propensity.

[26] For example, Ludwig's (2005) position is that it is not nature which brings about perpetual peace, but political agents; all that nature guarantees, according to Ludwig, is that the success of political action aimed at perpetual peace is not ruled out from the very beginning or in principle.

over the years.[27] The suggestion that the difference simply boils down to whether the model does or does not subscribe to the identity thesis according to which each appearance is numerically identical with a thing in itself cannot be correct. Plainly, since things in themselves do not have spatiotemporal properties they are not numerically identical to any appearance. The TA view, properly conceived, must maintain that appearances form something like composite wholes with things in themselves, although it remains to be seen how this idea can be spelt out in detail, for example, in terms of different types of properties. Along this line, the term "human being" ("Mensch") may indicate such a composite whole, one in which a human being as a sense entity is but one element, feature or part constituted by its properties that are open to sensory intuition. Kant's language in this sentence clearly suggests that there is something about the human being over and beyond nature and that may be exempted from the mechanism of nature.

His focus on "sense entity," however, appears to support the view that freedom is lacking here, because in the world of the senses, causal laws reign, and this view generates a remarkable tension with the notion of duty that Kant repeatedly invokes with regard to perpetual peace.

2.4.1 Providence and Nature

As far as Kant's point about the "form of nature" and its connection to the "end of a world author" is concerned, one would initially think that "form" here refers to the structure of the sphere of appearances explored in the transcendental aesthetic and the analytic of the first *Critique*, in particular to the world's spatio-temporality, the fact that space and time are forms of (human, sensory) intuition and are subject to the principles of the pure understanding, in particular the analogies of experience. However, since Kant connects this "form of nature" to the notion of God, he most probably has what we could call the *specific lawfulness* of the sphere of appearances in mind (by virtue of the special laws that are valid therein), because as we know from both his account of the regulative use of (ideas of) reason (e.g., CPR A670f./B698f.) and from the introduction to the third *Critique* (CJ 5: 180f.), the validity of specific laws of nature and their yielding a system accessible to human cognition is accounted for with reference to a divine, intuitive intellect.

In reference to "specific lawfulness" the term "specific" is not meant to be opposed to "general" – specific laws are of course also expressed by general propositions. Rather, specific laws are understood as being contrasted with the principles of the understanding, such as the principle of causality or the second

---

[27] See Ertl (2016) for a brief sketch.

analogy of experience. An example of a specific natural law would be the law of gravitation. In the realm of the specific laws there are, therefore, different levels with the law of gravitation being perhaps the most basic specific law of nature. As we shall see, specific laws of nature and their metaphysical profile in terms of modality are important for solving one aspect of the problem of freedom in Kant.

Furthermore, Kant speaks about "predetermining," or perhaps more cautiously "determining beforehand" ("vorher bestimmen") this form, and "determining," as Kant maintained since his *Nova Dilucidatio* (1755), can be epistemic and constitutive (NE 1: 391–393). In a constitutive sense the term "to determine" is often used in the passive voice, that is, "to be determined" which means that an entity is this rather than that, A rather than non-A. In the active voice and when it comes to the epistemic sense, the term indicates that somebody gets to know that an entity is this rather than that by virtue of what is often called its (epistemic) determining ground or *ratio cognoscendi*. "To determine" in the constitutive sense, taken in the active voice, means that something, that is, the determining ground in a constitutive sense (the *ratio essendi vel fiendi*), is turning an entity into this rather than that. Most importantly, "determining," in this sense, should not be read along the lines of modern conceptions of determinism. Rather, the determining ground in the constitutive sense can in principle be a free agent as well, as is obvious in the very case of God under consideration. Our text says: The form of nature is connected to the end of the creator insofar as this form can only be rendered intelligible in connection with this end, presumably insofar as it plays a role in realizing this end. Hence, Kant's point is that God grasps what this form is or has to be like "before" the existence of nature (in which case the form is in some sense there, albeit uninstantiated), but it can also mean that the form of nature (in the sense indicated) is due to the world author for the end in question.

The "before" is most naturally taken in a temporal sense, but it can also express merely logical priority. One of the main tasks in the remainder of this Element will be to investigate in which way epistemic and constitutive dimensions are involved when it comes to the world author as the determining ground of the form of the world. There is no question that when Kant invokes a world author in the first place, that author is thought to be responsible for the existence or actuality of everything apart from said author and hence also for the existence of nature and its form. Our question will be about the extent of the discretion the world author has with regard to the specifics or the particular shape of this form. Plainly, this issue is closely connected to the question concerning the agency by which the end of the world author, and indeed the entire cascade of ends subordinate to it, is supposed to come about after all.

The interpretation of "form of nature" in the sense of specific lawfulness goes together well with Kant's definition of providence in reply, and in contrast, to

Baumgarten. For Kant, providence is the implementation of the (specific) laws of nature according to which the course of nature was supposed to proceed.[28] As we shall see, this definition provides one of the clues to Kant's identification (in a sense to be specified and qualified in further detail) of providence and nature as the guarantor of perpetual peace, and providence, in turn, will be revealed as the key device in Kant for securing freedom in the face of the specific laws of nature that are valid in the world of senses.

The "end of a world author" is surely the objective ultimate end of creation mentioned in the main text (briefly discussed above) and corresponding to *finis creationis*, a topic which Kant usually discussed in his metaphysics lectures and lectures on natural theology. The pertinent paragraphs in Baumgarten's *Metaphysica*, which served as the main textbook for these courses, are M §§942–949 in Part IV, Chapter II on *Operationes Dei*. For Kant, in line with what has been said about moral self-perfection above, the core element of this end is the morally correct use of freedom on the part of the created beings (PhilTh-P 28: 1099). Moreover, in the lectures Kant distinguishes the objective from the subjective end of creation, the subjective end being what God gains from the whole enterprise of creation (PhilTh-P 28: 1099).

Kant's statements in the lectures associate closely the *finis creationis* with the highest derivative good, as developed mainly in CPrR (5: 125–132), whereas in the CJ (5: 435) Kant explicitly says that "the human being, though considered as noumenon" is the final end of creation. With regard to the highest derivative good, Kant distinguishes an unconditional and a conditional element, namely, morality or "virtue," that is, the "supreme good" (CPrR 5: 110) and proportionate happiness, respectively. Corresponding to this, his remarks in CJ (5: 436fn) suggest that the objective ultimate end of creation, properly speaking, is concerned with the unconditional aspect of the highest derivative good. That this cannot mean the human being insofar as such a human is merely *capable* of being morally good[29] is made clear by Kant in CJ §§84–86; here, he stresses the role the human good will, as determined by itself and as providing (the supreme condition of) the objective determining ground for the divine act of creation (5: 443) so that the human being, insofar as such a human *has* a good will, is the objective ultimate end, properly speaking. When used on its own in order to indicate the end of creation, the expression "human being" therefore needs to be understood in an emphatic sense, stressing the actualization of the capacity to be morally good. This, in line with Baumgarten's criticism (M §875) of the

---

[28] See, for example, PhilTh-P 28: 1110, in reference to Baumgarten (M §975).

[29] In this respect, I agree with Dean (2012: 243fn5), but unlike Dean I take it that these passages in CJ are consistent with this claim.

Socinians[30] who denied divine foreknowledge of future, free human actions and who Kant mentions disapprovingly in Th-B (28: 1271), strongly suggests that for Kant God knows about the outcome of his putative creative activity, knows that it is positive and hence sets the whole scheme in motion. In section 3, I shall return to this issue in more detail.

Kant's proviso, namely, that the human being is the end of creation "considered as noumenon" raises an important further issue. Put simply, is the human being the end of creation as an embodied noumenon or as a separate substance? Echoing a debate about the highest good, an alternative way of asking this question is whether moralization is supposed to occur in an "immanent" or "transcendent" manner.[31] Connected to this, and as indicated above, Kant's formulation "the human being" also leaves it open as to whether each and every human being or just a limited number of them are supposed to be the objective ultimate end of creation in the sense indicated.

Yet another layer of paradox emerges here: Talking about a "form of nature" implies treating humans as natural entities, while the master end of creation has to do with their freedom which exists only outside of nature, although, again, freedom can be taken as having effects in nature. This is true of both the immanent and the transcendent reading. Kant clearly suggests, though, that the natural dimension plays an integral and vital part or role for the final end which has an extranatural core. To be sure, and to complicate matters even further, this realm external to nature has its own – as I shall say – facet or even facets of the freedom problem related to creation and grace, as we shall see below.

Kant continues in the footnote as follows:

> whose *predetermination* we call (divine) providence as such, and, insofar as it is put in the *beginning* of the world the *grounding one* (*providentia conditrix; semel iussit, semper parent*, Augustin) . . . (TPP 8: 361.8–11fn, my translation)

Here, to be sure, "providence" is defined as "predetermination of the form of nature," but this, in line with what has just been said above, can easily be taken to be equivalent to the definition in the theology lectures. Kant is basically making the same point in slightly more abstract terms. Predetermination in the sense of rendering the grasped or produced form actual simply amounts to the implementation of the laws of nature, which in turn confirms or at least supports

---

[30] The Socinians, followers of Laelius Socinus, were a sixteenth-century rationalist Christian movement particularly strong in Poland. In their denial of divine human foreknowledge of future, free human actions they are akin to the open theists of our time, such as Richard Rice.

[31] This is Silber's (1959) terminology. In an influential paper Reath (1988) claimed that Kant shifted from a transcendent to an immanent notion of the highest good in his later years. For a critical discussion of this claim, see Pasternack (2017).

the reading of "form" as specific lawfulness of nature. As we have seen above, one important question will be to what extent merely epistemic elements are in play with regard to God determining this form apart from rendering it actual (in which respect his determination is clearly constitutive).

Kant is also discussing several different aspects or perhaps even types of providence (TPP 8: 361.10–39fn), but for lack of space I cannot deal with these here. An important distinction which Kant does not mention, but which is crucial for our purposes, is the distinction between the object sense and the process sense of the term "providence." "Providence," and this is even clearer with regard to the systematically equivocal German term "Vorsehung," can be an act on the part of God and also the effect or the result of such an act. At any rate, while this distinction between the object sense and the process sense of "providence" does not fully coincide with the formal–material distinction of providence Kant endorses in TPP 8: 361.23–28fn, nature (and 'nature' in the formal sense at that) can, in some respects at least, obviously be regarded as providence in the object sense, that is, as the result of a divine activity. As we have seen, the primary 'results' of the activity of providence are the special laws of nature which, together with, for example, the principles of the understanding, make up the form of nature. As Kant clarifies in other passages, such as G 4: 437, the connection of things according to general laws is that which constitutes the formal aspect of nature. This identification of nature in the formal sense as indicated, and providence in the object sense, is an important result in its own right, and helps us better understand Kant's initially apparently unclear position as to what after all is the guarantor power of perpetual peace. Clearly, this identification works only when a perspective unifying the theoretical and practical points of view is adopted.

There is a further important aspect to this identification of nature and providence in the sense indicated, and this has to do with the puzzling and much discussed personification of nature by Kant.[32] In his classic account of providence – setting the conceptual framework for centuries to come – Aquinas (in SThIaqu22art3corp) claimed that God delegated providence in the sense of the execution of the implemented "order of things" to lower-ranked intelligent created entities (different from human persons). When talking about nature "wanting" and having purposes and the like (e.g., TPP 8: 365, 367) – in short, when treating nature as a person – Kant is alluding to this tradition, although presumably not directly to Aquinas. It is nature which has taken over the task of looking after the created entities and Kant's metaphor or personification may, on the one hand, be said to simply reiterate and emphasize this function of nature.

---

[32] See Kleingeld (2001) for a discussion of the pertinent passages.

On the other hand, Kant may wish to undercut the need for an intelligent entity different from nature to do this. Paradoxically, then, rather than literally ascribing propositional attitudes to nature, the personification of nature has the purpose of indicating that no metaphysically obscure intelligent entities are needed to carry out the oversight over creation on God's behalf.

Admittedly, Kant is nonetheless quite careful in the guarantee footnote; he speaks of "indicating the provision of a wisdom in charge of nature" (TPP 8: 361.39–41fn), and this does not suggest that the presence or actuality of providence can be *proven* by these observations. This seems entirely correct since the situation sketched by Kant could in principle be described the other way around: People are living in such and such locations, simply because they saw the Gulf Stream providing the indispensable wood. In this case, however, the "end" of getting people there would still be achieved, if there were such an "end" in the first place, of course. In line with what has been said above we should not read Kant here as arguing for the existence of such "a wisdom." The point must rather be that Kant takes the postulates of pure practical reason and the doctrine of a regulative use of reason for granted and is now trying to spell out the implications of these doctrines in more detail. In any event, the strategy Kant pursues here is indicative of his idea of a correlation between mechanical and teleological explanations, in terms of an instrumentalist conception according to which the mechanical explanation can be embedded into a more complex story involving ends through reference to an intelligent cause behind the world. To be sure, for Kant, the reference to such an intelligent cause has no use in scientific explanations of phenomena in the world in space and time.

It is perhaps helpful to sum up the points half way through this remarkable footnote. What emerges here in the first half of our footnote is an idea often inaccurately attributed to Hegel,[33] but which can be found in scholastic texts such as Aquinas' *Summa de Theologia* (Iaqu14art5–16), namely, God's thoughts before the creation and subsequent actions, insofar as he is contemplating how to shape the world in order to realize his goal. Most strikingly, in the case of Kant, however, this end involves something created rational agents need to and can do essentially only by themselves, namely, their moral self-perfection. Hence, while providence aka nature seems to take agency away from created rational agents, the overall aim of the entire activity of creation is,

---

[33] In the pertinent passage, namely, the introduction to the *Science of Logic*, Hegel (2000: 29) himself says: "Accordingly, logic is to be understood as the system of pure reason, as the realm of pure thought. *This realm is truth unveiled, truth as it is in and for itself.* It can therefore be said that this content is *the exposition of God as he is in his eternal essence before the creation of nature and of a finite spirit.*" In contrast to Kant's approach, Hegel's God is not engaged in any deliberations about the word.

in turn, entrusted to these finite rational agents. The question remains whether Kant has the adequate instruments for tackling this obvious tension.

2.4.2 Concursus *and Nature*

In the second half of the footnote, Kant draws on a number of classic terms in order to elucidate how to understand the interplay of created rational agents and God with regard to their respective roles in setting the world on track for these ends. He emphasizes that the type of interaction between God and causes in the world of space and time must not be regarded as a case of *concursus*, and this claim – as we will see – complements his ideas about providence discussed above. On the moral scale, however, Kant is prepared to accept such a *concursus* which, in turn, adds the complication of a further threat to human freedom, and a threat on the level of things in themselves at that. Let us proceed step by step again. Kant says:

> Only as far as the concept, common in the schools, of a divine *joining in* or collaboration (*concursus*) to an effect in the world of sense is concerned, this is to be omitted here. Wanting to pair the inhomogeneous (*gryphes iungere equis*), and to have him who is himself the complete cause of the changes in the world, *complement* his own predetermining providence (which therefore would have to have been deficient) during the course of the world, for example, to say that the physician *besides God* has set the sick right, hence had been involved as support, is *firstly* inconsistent in itself. For *causa solitaria non iuvat*. God is the originator of the physician (along with all his remedies), and hence, if one does wish to ascend to the highest fundamental ground, theoretically unknown to us, the effect has to be ascribed to him *in full*. (TPP 8: 361.39–362.28fn, my translation)

According to Kant, the notion of *concursus* does not apply with regard to God in relation to effects in the sensual world, even though *providence* does, and when taken in the object sense, as we have just seen, is in turn nothing but nature in the formal sense. Assuming that God and natural causes did concur, this would amount to connecting categorically different entities, as the image of eagles and horses being harnessed together dramatically illustrates. In line with what has been said above, this can best be understood as maintaining that both God and the physician (the latter taken together with his remedies and, of course, several other factors such as temperature etc.) are each sufficient for the recovery of the patient; and that *concursus* only occurs between causes (or a plurality of causes) which by themselves are not sufficient to bring about the effect in question. In this vein, speaking of sufficient causes as concurring would indeed amount to a contradiction. In fact, Kant's understanding of *concursus* can be elucidated via John Mackie's similar conception of causality and I shall try to get back to this issue in a moment.[34] In the passage under consideration, Kant illustrates the idea of sufficiency in terms of the lack of shortcomings in God's own providence. We would have to concede these shortcomings, if the natural causes were insufficient. Note that in the above, providence was defined in terms of determination, which has both an epistemic and a constitutive meaning. Here, its constitutive meaning (at least in the sense of rendering these causes actual) is pertinent. Had God arranged the causes in a way that required his constant help to render them sufficient, his determination would indeed have been defective. Creating causes which then do all the causal work in space and time is not a case of *concursus*, but of mere conservationism.

Concurrentism is opposed to mere conservationism and indicates a different form of cooperation between God and causes in the world.[35] For our further discussion, it is helpful to look into these matters in more detail. As indicated, and put simply, *concursus* is the cooperation of a number of causes to bring about an effect (see M §314). This is first and foremost a general account, similar perhaps to ideas underlying Mackie's (1974) theory of causality according to which the cause of an effect under scrutiny "is an insufficient, but necessary component in a bundle of factors that was unnecessary, but sufficient for the occurrence" of it (Loux 2006: 197).[36] To be sure, *concursus* should not be thought of in terms of a number of different actions, but in terms of causes working together to produce one action. In contrast to Mackie, therefore, all (or at least several) factors of the bundle can count as causes in *concursus*. In line with Mackie, however, causes are not by themselves sufficient conditions for an effect to occur. Also, *concursus* is usually meant to apply to efficient causality and this also holds for what follows; however, in principle nothing stands in the way of applying it, for example, to the other three in the Aristotelian list. In any event, within classical theism (for example, Baumgarten in M §§958–962) this general account of *concursus* can and has been applied to the special case of divine *concursus*. Here, the issue is the interplay of God as the first cause, and created causes as secondary causes, bringing about an effect.

For the sake of clarification, I shall use 'cooperation' as the wider concept and 'concurrence' as the narrower concept in the following: Mere conservationists restrict divine cooperation to creation and conservation of the secondary causes (and of the true substances whose states can count as effects of secondary

---

[34] In general, what Kant says in the guarantee footnote also coheres well with Eric Watkins' (2005) claim that for Kant causes are substances, not event tokens as often assumed. In this regard, Kant is, therefore, Aristotelian rather than Davidsonian.

[35] In my account of concurrentism above I am reusing – partially verbatim – material from Ertl (2017b). I should like to thank the editors of *Critique* for their kind permission to do so.

[36] See Rosefeldt (2012: 104–106) for a more detailed discussion of *concursus* in terms of Mackie's so-called "INUS-account" of causality.

causes), while concurrentists think that divine causal cooperation involves more than this.

The doctrine of *concursus* has been investigated in full detail by Alfred Freddoso (1988a, 1988b, 1991, 1994, 2002)[37], on whom I shall basically rely in this account. As Freddoso has shown, almost everyone involved in the pertinent mediæval and early modern discussions subscribed to the creation and conservation thesis, namely, that the substances in the universe, which might qualify as causes apart from God, have been created by God *ex nihilo* and are sustained in existence or conserved at any moment in time through God. It is important and illuminating to see that the generally perhaps more well-known doctrine of occasionalism can (at least in part) be accounted for against the background of the problem of cooperation. In a sense, occasionalism is at one (extreme) end of the spectrum of possible positions, simply by denying cooperation on the part of created entities. The occasionalists (such as Al-Ghazali, Nicolas of Autrecourt and, later, of course, Malebranche) think that God is the only (genuine) efficient cause in the universe. While God is the creator of the entities which make up the world and sustains them in existence, none of these entities contribute causally (in the sense of a genuine efficient cause) to what is going on in the world.

However, in the mediæval and early modern accounts of cooperation it was generally assumed that the created causes *do contribute causally* (as efficient causes) to changes in the world. There are, however, a number of very different views as to how this contribution works. These are the already mentioned positions of *mere conservationism*, on the one hand, and *concurrentism* on the other. In a sense, mere conservationism is diametrically opposed to occasionalism and hence at the opposite end of the spectrum of possible positions. A mere conservationist claims that divine cooperation is restricted to creation and conservation of the created causes, while the created causes themselves do all the work of bringing about change in the world.

Mere conservationism, however, as has been pointed out recently,[38] was a fringe position in the mediæval and early modern debate about cooperation. Most of the scholastics were concurrentists and assumed that God does indeed play a more active role than this, that is, being involved in bringing about the changes in the world as well, adding something to the activity of created causes in this respect.

There are, however, at least two very different versions of concurrentism that have been developed by philosophers and theologians who claim that God's cooperation with secondary causes goes beyond mere creating and conserving

---

[37] See also Hogan (forthcoming).   [38] Insole (2015: 202).

them. These versions are built on different models of how God's activity exceeds the creation and conservation of the substances.

These are, on the one hand, the Aquinian model, or at any rate the model used by Thomists in the ensuing debates. This model involves the idea that God acts *on*, or perhaps better, provides a causal contribution to the secondary causes, and that this activity is required to release their causal power. When it comes to rational agents, this divine contribution to secondary or created causes has somewhat polemically been called *praedeterminatio* or *praemotio* (see Hübener 1989). In short, God premoves the will of a rational agent to render it active. On the other hand, a quite different account has been provided by Molina, according to whom God acts, or perhaps better, provides a causal contribution, *along* with the finite causes or *together* with them.

Most importantly, and in clear contrast to Kant's position, neither for the Thomists nor for the Molinists can created causes on their own ever be *sufficient* to bring about an effect in the world of space and time. In this vein, a denial of concurrentism for the world in space and time is indispensable as a core feature of Kant's theoretical philosophy. If one indeed wishes to use these doctrines to shed light on Kant's thinking, an important point to make is that, assuming that Kant opts for a theist stance in one way or another, mere conservationism is required in connection with what I have labelled above as the 'methodologically naturalist' dimension of transcendental idealism. Kant is adamant that events in the world of appearances can, and indeed must, be accounted for by natural science, and this, plainly, presupposes that natural causes can be sufficient for bringing about an effect in this realm.

God and natural causes each being sufficient to bring about the effect raises the problem of freedom – for example, concerning the actions of the physician. In fact, at least two compatibility issues arise, namely, about the freedom of the physician in the light of God creating him, and the freedom of the physician in the light of natural causes being sufficient for the outcome. We will examine this problem below. In the passages discussed so far, though, Kant clearly treats the physician and his actions as natural entities, and insofar as they are natural entities, freedom does not apply to them. This does not solve the freedom problem nor render it obsolete; it just arises in a different context. The question, in short, is how these actions can *also* be free, and this question shall be investigated in section 3.

The idea that sufficient causes or sets of sufficient causes do not cooperate also explains Kant's remark that a single cause does not "help" (TPP 8: 25–26); assuming that there is a single *sufficient* cause (*causa solitaria*) it does not help or contribute to bringing about an effect, but brings it about all by itself or on its own. "Help" plainly requires something or some entity or agent to be helped.

Kant is not speaking here about the problem of overdetermination, but has something different in mind, namely, what he sometimes calls the "subordination" (PhilTh-P 28: 1106) of causes in a series of causes. In one form of subordination, A is sufficient for B and B is sufficient for C. In this case, there is no *concursus* between A and B with respect to bringing about C, but by virtue of bringing about B, A brings about C.

The text of the footnote continues as follows:

> Or one can also *completely* ascribe it to the physician, insofar as we trace this event as explicable according to the order of nature in the chain of world causes. (TPP 8: 362. 28–30fn, my translation)

Again, it is obvious that for Kant, natural causes or "world causes," as he says here, can (in their combination) be sufficient for bringing about an effect. Clearly, though, Kant must mean "the physician and his remedies and several other factors," as indicated above. Kant now discusses a second problem which would arise were we to assume a *concursus* of God and natural causes with respect to events in nature:

> *Secondly*, such a way of thinking deprives us of all determinate principles of the assessment of an effect. (TPP 8: 362.30–32fn, my translation)

It is particularly difficult to tell what Kant is trying to get at here. The first thought which comes to mind is perhaps that he is thinking about moral responsibility: Under the assumption of concurring *sufficient* causes, it is unclear who or what is responsible for the effect. However, and as indicated – at least as far as the physician is concerned – Kant is talking about the order of nature in which freedom has no place. One possible reading, therefore, is as follows: Assuming that two causes are each sufficient for bringing about the effect, it is impossible to say due to which cause the effect as a whole is occurring or what each is bringing about in the effect, while in the case in which insufficient causes work together the situation may be different. If two physicians (and their remedies and other supporting factors) brought the patient back to health, one may have stabilized the blood pressure while the other perhaps provided an antidote to a poison.

2.4.3 Moral Self-Perfection and Grace

Kant now makes what – on the face of it – looks like a surprising concession:

> But in a *moral-practical* respect (which hence is completely directed to the supersensual), for example, in the faith that God will supplement the deficiency of our own justice also through means incomprehensible to us, if only our fundamental disposition has been genuine, and we therefore shall not loosen anything in our effort toward the good, the concept of a divine

concursus is quite seemly and even necessary; in which it goes without saying, of course, that nobody must try to *explain* a good action (as an event in the world) out of this, which is a presumed knowledge of the supersensual, hence absurd. (TPP 8: 362.32–39fn, my translation)

Kant here alludes to the issue of grace – treated by him at length in the second piece of the *Religion* – and locates its workings beyond the sphere of nature. In line with what has been said above regarding the TA model of the distinction between things in themselves and appearances, if grace is something given to an embodied agent, the object of grace must still be the human being taken as thing in itself, although this raises difficult questions as to how the atemporality of things in themselves can be squared with the notion of something occurring there. In any event, Kant appears to be saying that the bringing about of a human agent's true justice can indeed involve "codetermination" ("Mitbestimmung", see Ameriks 2016: 219) and hence a plurality of causes (each of which not sufficient by itself), namely, mainly the human agent in question and God. While in contrast to the situation in nature, Kant clearly suggests a concurrentist position in the moral realm, he does not elaborate which form of concurrentism (an Aquinian, a Molinist conception or some other form) he has in mind.

When it comes to grace, the Thomist model is in any event, at least in principle, the one suitable for the *concursus* involved here, since in this regard the finite agent must in some way be the 'recipient' of divine activity, and even Molina subscribed to this version in this context, albeit with an important twist: In the context of grace, Molina (*Concordia* III, 41) does indeed switch to the Thomist model but disagrees with the Thomists about the scope of divine power. When it comes to grace, God's causal contribution indeed relates to the human agent qua potential cause but, for Molina, *human* cooperation is needed for *divine* grace to unfold its potential, which a fortiori means that lack of human cooperation 'blocks' the efficacy of divine grace. In other words, while the granting of grace through God is necessary for salvation, it is not sufficient. In Molina's account, neither human cooperation nor the lack of it can be 'overwritten' or compensated for by God. Put somewhat dramatically, the human capacity of cooperation is beyond the reach of divine power, and this, in turn, is precisely where human freedom predominantly manifests itself. In this manner, Molina places humans and God on the same level with regard to their freedom – a truly revolutionary claim, from a most unlikely source.

Anyway, in our footnote Kant insists that we must not draw on God's provision of this supplement for an explanation of a good, and this is in line with all we know about Kant's moral theory, a free action.

Grace is, of course, concerned with the moral perfection of the agents, and if it is indeed a duty to morally perfect oneself, grace must not undermine freedom. Moreover, should the coming about of perpetual peace presuppose self-perfection, the issue of grace and its compatibility with freedom directly concerns perpetual peace as well.

Summing up the gist of the second half of the guarantee footnote it is fair to say that Kant completes his account of the compatibility of divine causal involvement with the world and methodological naturalism, by dispersing possible worries that the acceptance of providence commits us to what we could call a "prescientific stance." Surprisingly enough, though, a key element of such a prescientific stance, namely, the thesis of there being a *concursus* between a first and secondary rational agents, is conceded on the level of things in themselves by Kant.[39]

2.5 Contexts

I should like to end this section with a very brief attempt at a contextual reading of the passages considered above indicating how they connect to other passages in Kant's œuvre,[40] partly reiterating what has been said above already.

Among Kant's published texts the guarantee addendum provides the most comprehensive account of concepts concerning divine actions with regard to events in the world, and this account roughly corresponds to parts of the section "*Operationes Dei*" (i.e., §§926–981) in Baumgarten's *Metaphysica*. Only the theology lectures (e.g., PhilTh-P 28: 1091–1117) and the theology parts of the metaphysics lectures – and here the Dohna-Wundlacken 4 notes of lectures held in 1792–3 are the closest in terms of chronology and with a surviving, albeit in this case comparatively brief, theology part (see 28: 690–702) – are more detailed.[41]

A further important feature of the passages discussed above is that they involve a twofold cross-reference with key passages of the *Critique of the Power of Judgement* (1790) and of the *Religion* (1793), the two monographs

---

[39] It is a fair point to ask whether the doctrines about providence and cooperation belong to doctrinal or moral belief, as classified in CPR A820/B848–A831/B859. Following Baiasu's (2018: 193–197) lead, it is true that mere conservationism, for example, and the subscription to the creation thesis this involves, may also be available as an object of *doctrinal* belief in Kant, namely, within the regulative use of reason. But since what matters here is Kant's "moral 'creationism'," as Karl Ameriks (2012: 238) has put it, I take it that moral belief is pertinent. Similar to what Baiasu has maintained about the guarantee thesis, we can perhaps say that mere creationism and providence enter practically grounded metaphysics as an object of doctrinal belief, but receive their moral direction through the moral belief in God's objective ultimate end. In any event, and as Ameriks (2012: 246) has emphasized, for Kant – strikingly enough – moral belief seems to rank higher than knowledge in CJ §91.

[40] To be sure, this overview does not include the normative side of Kant's doctrine of perpetual peace.

[41] The final part of this section in Baumgarten (namely, M §§982–1000 that discusses providence "through revelation") is arguably dealt with in the *Religion*, in particular, in those sections which discuss the problem of how to deal with the Scriptures in rational religion (Rel 6: 102–114).

of Kant preceding the essay *Perpetual Peace*. In addition to presupposing the moral argument, in particular, in its CJ version (5: 447–453), the pertinent sections there are marked by a similar, or perhaps better, reverse difficulty. While it is at least not immediately obvious why Kant mentions the concept of a cosmopolitan legal condition (see CJ 5: 432) in a context primarily concerned with natural teleology which, in turn, is preparatory to arguing for a practically grounded metaphysics, the difficulty in the guarantee addendum is the recourse to practically grounded metaphysics in a context primarily concerned with issues of philosophy of law and history. The second cross-reference is to passages in the *Religion* where Kant's ideas about grace (e.g., Rel 6: 71–78, 190–192) and his normative claims about the ethical commonwealth (e.g., Rel 6: 94–95) correspond to the conception of concurrentism endorsed in the guarantor footnote.

Arguably, the cross-reference to the final section of the third *Critique* is part of an elaborate double strategy. The connoisseurs of the critical project will of course have been aware of the last words in a work with which the critical business is supposed to have come to an end (see CJ 5: 170), while the non-connoisseurs have been invited to consider Kant's finely balanced position with regard to practically grounded metaphysics developed there.[42] In the guarantee addendum he raises expectations with regard to the guarantee of perpetual peace only to 'disappoint' them by admitting that theory on its own with its focus on nature as the guarantor power cannot live up to such expectations. At the same time, he provides the material on the basis of which the expectations can be met, but only in the downscaled mode of practical cognition and without explaining why this is the case.

It is, of course, striking that this strategy is deployed in a text predominantly concerned with matters of politics and history. While it is true that the issue of peace is first and foremost a political goal, Kant provides at least clues as to how this goal fits into a much bigger picture we can paint about the world from a practical perspective. When it comes to the issue of a guarantee for peace, which again is a political *topos*, and to a guarantee writ large in the case of perpetual peace, this bigger picture can provide the means to establish such a comprehensive guarantee, as we shall see in section 4. Within such a bigger picture, not available solely on theoretical grounds, perpetual peace is but an intermediary end to be brought about by us on the basis of something like

---

[42] Kant's repeated move of drawing on the notion of an objective ultimate end of a world author, although transcending the realm of theory, also reiterates his carefully calibrated anti-Spinozist standpoint emphasized, for example, in CJ (5: 452–453) where he says that Spinoza's assumption must weaken respect for the moral law even in a righteous person like Spinoza himself. For a comprehensive account of Kant's criticism of Spinoza, see Boehm (2014).

political skills in the use of the mechanism of nature for this end by the "world author." Before turning to this issue, however, we need to look at the problem of freedom, since Kant's attempted solution elsewhere in his œuvre will turn out to be useful for understanding his position in this regard.

3 The Guarantor Powers and Freedom

In the previous section, we saw how the guarantor powers are connected and how Kant describes the interplay of various types of causes with regard to processes pertinent to perpetual peace. The key sentence in the guarantee addendum about the form of nature and its determination (TPP 8: 361.5–8fn) could be used to establish the identity of providence in an object sense of the term and nature in the formal sense of it from the perspective of the unity of practical and theoretical reason.

In this section, I will first distinguish the different facets of the problem of freedom which arise by virtue of the account given so far of how the guarantor powers work. I shall then sketch Kant's stance on the question of how the natural causal determinism underlying the mechanism of nature is compatible with the kind of freedom underlying moral obligation and try to show that this stance is the focal point of Kant's position with regard to compatibility *tout court*. For Kant, human freedom, for all its contingency, has a bedrock character. It is – within practically grounded metaphysics – ontologically prior both to nature and, presumably, in an important sense even to divine agency as well.

3.1 Facets of the Problem of Freedom

The notion of entrusting nature to divine planning – maintained, strange as it initially seems, by the critical Kant – certainly strengthens the idea that there may be something like a guarantee of perpetual peace. Anything involving duty, however, presupposes freedom, be it the core of the objective ultimate end or working towards perpetual peace.

However, the account of the world given so far, with regard to both appearances and things in themselves, is on the face of it rather difficult to square with the freedom of the finite rational agents.[43] All the models of cooperation suggested by Kant, mere conservationism for nature and concurrentism for morality, are afflicted with this problem; yet, in the main text of the guarantee addendum Kant says:

---

[43] Ypi (2010: 142), for example, rejects a future actuality reading of the guarantee thesis because of Kant's very commitment to human freedom, while Baiasu (2018: 190) rightly emphasizes Kant's endorsement of the compatibility thesis in this regard.

> Now the question which concerns the essence of aiming for perpetual peace is: "What nature does in this aiming or concerning the end which his own reason renders into a duty for the human being, hence for the furthering of his *moral aim*, and how it provides this liability, so that what the human being *should* do according to laws of freedom, but does not do, is ensured that he will do it with this freedom unscathed, also through a coercion of nature, and according to all three proportions of public law at that, of *state, international* and *cosmopolitan law*." – When I say of nature, it wants this or that to happen, this does not mean as much as: It imposes a duty on us to do it (because this only coercion-free practical reason is able to), but it does it itself, we may want to or not (*fata volentem ducunt, nolentem trahunt*). (TPP 8: 365.20–32, my translation)

The question we need to ask now plainly is: How can this freedom of the human agent (by virtue of which it can be a duty to work for perpetual peace) indeed remain "unscathed," given the picture that emerges in the footnote of a predominantly divine agency that acts both with nature being subordinate to it and in a way that extends to a sphere beyond nature. As much as the guarantee addendum helps us penetrate more deeply into the practically grounded metaphysics sustaining Kant's claims with regard to politics and history, it does not reveal all its intricate details.

In order to address the problem of human freedom, it is indeed crucial to distinguish different threats to this freedom. When speaking about 'threats' I simply take this as a short form for saying that certain truths or, more cautiously, claims (for example, in theoretical philosophy) render it difficult to see how the freedom thesis can be upheld with regard to human beings.

We need to properly differentiate threats that emerge from God and threats that emerge from elsewhere – for example, from the activity of causes in the world of nature, which from a theological perspective is the realm of created causes, even though these created causes may follow divinely enacted special natural laws.

On the part of God, we can distinguish the following three potential threats:

(1) His knowledge about our (future) acts might undercut the freedom of these acts. We can call this the *(fore)knowledge facet of the problem of freedom*.
(2) His causal activity of creation and conservation might undercut the freedom of human acts due to the radical ontological dependency of human agents this may be seen to involve. Accordingly, we can speak of an *ontological dependency facet of the problem of freedom*.
(3) His causal activity in the world in addition to creation and conservation (as the concurrentists have it) might undercut the freedom of our acts. This primarily concerns the issue of grace in the account of concurrentism

sketched above. Hence, there is something like a *divine contribution, involvement* or, indeed, a *concurrence facet of the problem of freedom.* Plainly, if one really thinks that God does more than merely create and sustain the free causes in existence, then the question arises as to whether this doing more is compatible with the freedom of these causes and their actions.

On the part of causes other than God, the following threats to human freedom emerge:

(4) The causal activity of causes in the natural world different from God might be undercutting the freedom of the human agent. These activities could be both internal and external to the agent, and this threat can come in at least two variants, namely: (a) in the form of the natural causal determinism thesis discussed widely in the contemporary debate about the problem of freedom, with van Inwagen (1983: 56) providing perhaps the standard definition or account of this thesis to which I shall return below; (b) in the form of coercion through natural causes. Clearly, (a) and (b) do not amount to one and the same thing. While coercion is perhaps thought to be more obviously incompatible with freedom, the situation is very different with regard to the determinism thesis. Some compatibilists have argued that one might mistakenly take the determinism thesis to be incompatible with freedom because of an unwarranted identification of determinism and coercion. Strikingly, Kant does indeed speak of "coercion of nature" (TPP 8: 365.25–26, my translation) and of "compulsion" (TPP 8: 360.16, my translation) with regard to fate and we shall have to enquire how to understand this surprising move and how such a coercion, in particular, can possibly leave human freedom "unscathed." The difference between determinism and coercion notwithstanding, we can speak of a *natural causal facet of the freedom problem.*

There are even further possible threats to human freedom, which are not necessarily linked to causality; for example, a threat arising from the nature of truth:

(5) One might wish to argue that the mere truth-aptness of propositions about future human acts is incompatible with their freedom. This is, of course, a different issue from the one arising in the context of perfect divine knowledge. One can call this the *logical* or *truth-theoretical facet of the problem of human freedom.* This is a topic widely discussed in the wake of Aristotle's famous example of a future sea battle in *De interpretatione* I.9, but for Kant this problem is something which he does not even consider.

Truth-aptness as such does not undermine freedom for him. What matters is the issue in virtue of what there are these truths.

In the account in our footnote, facets (1)–(4) are clearly pertinent and, as we shall also see, (5) can at least be relevant in elucidating Kant's strategy.[44]

3.2 Kant's Altered Law Compatibilism

The problem of human freedom is one of the most widely and intensely discussed problems in philosophy, and this also holds for Kant's treatment of it. Of particular importance is the so-called "compatibility question," that is, the very question as to whether human freedom can be upheld in the face of the threats it faces, and we have identified five of those threats in the previous section. In Kant's œuvre, his endorsement of compatibility holds the two main parts of his philosophy together, as it were. In the CPrR (5: 4fn), he even calls transcendental freedom the *ratio essendi* of the categorical imperative.

As mentioned before, Kant, in the guarantee addendum, takes the compatibility question as having been settled, but it is worth investigating the main outline of why he thinks he has the means available for establishing this compatibility. This is not only important in its own right, but getting clear about this will hopefully help us answer the question as to why Kant thinks he can assume that there is a guarantee of perpetual peace in the first place.

In doing so, I cannot enter a critical discussion of this vast topic, but only sketch the main outline of his approach. Some of the key building blocks of his solution will turn out to be instrumental with regard to this goal. While the previous section consisted of a close reading of key passages of the guarantor section of the essay *Perpetual Peace*, which tried to shed some light on what indeed looks like foreign bodies in a work mainly devoted to philosophy of history and the legal half of moral philosophy, we now need to move away from this text.

In Kant, the most important facet of the problem of freedom with regard to compatibility is undoubtedly facet (4), and the key text in Kant's works that addresses this issue is the solution to the third antinomy in the CPR (A532–A557/B560–B585).[45] With regard to facet (4) Kant needs to have the resources

---

[44] In my account of these facets I am drawing on Ertl (2017b); see footnote 35 above.

[45] It is striking that Kant mainly deals with the question of a free cause of the world in the thesis and antithesis of the third antinomy, while its resolution is concerned with human freedom, and facet (4) of it at that. It is contentious as to how these two topics are connected. Arguably, Kant's solution to facet (4) of the problem of human freedom can, within Kant's practically grounded

to undercut what is now considered to be the standard argument against compatibility, the so-called "consequence argument," developed by Peter van Inwagen. It must be said, however, that although Kant does not explicitly discuss this argument, it is widely agreed in the literature that it is the argument which needs to be defeated if compatibility is to be secured.

> (i) If determinism is true, then our acts are the consequences of the laws of nature and events in the remote past. (ii) But it is not up to us what went on before we were born, and neither is it up to us what the laws of nature are. (iii) Therefore the consequences of these things (including our present acts) are not up to us. (van Inwagen 1983: 56, numbering added)

This argument is meant to show that determinism and freedom or, to be more precise, the freedom thesis and the determinism thesis, are incompatible, that is, they cannot both be true. That they are incompatible is not a matter of course, which is often overlooked in discussions. Sometimes, establishing the determinism thesis is taken as amounting to a refutation of the freedom thesis, but this simply presupposes that both theses are incompatible, which is supposed to be shown in the first place.

Similarly, it is of no use for establishing compatibility to attack determinism. Moreover, it is important to point out that Kant's conception of freedom is not typically libertarian, while the consequence argument has originally been designed to attack such a symmetrical conception of freedom. Kant's position is asymmetrically libertarian, as one can perhaps put it (see MM 6: 226f.). This is to say, Kant holds that for an immoral action to be free the possibility of acting otherwise must be given, while this is not the case with regard to morally good actions. Since Kant clearly needs the claim that immoral actions are free, the argument does apply after all.

Now strikingly, premise (i) of this argument can be used in a very different manner or for an entirely different purpose, since if we take "our acts" to involve establishing perpetual peace, this captures the idea of a guarantee by virtue of the mechanism of nature very well.

Let us stay with the issue of the compatibility question, though, since – as mentioned before – some of the 'devices' to unseat the force of the consequence argument for incompatibility will give us a clue as to why the guarantee thesis holds for Kant. For premise (ii) to be false, at any rate, it is sufficient that the laws of nature *or* the distant past are in some sense at least up to us. The answer we can give on behalf of Kant to the consequence argument against compatibility – in a nutshell – is that, to a certain extent at least and as surprising as this

---

metaphysics, at least be elucidated or illustrated by issues related to creation, namely, through the idea of enacting special laws of nature, as we shall see below. See Ertl (2004) for further details.

may initially sound, it is in fact *up to us* what the laws of nature are. This is the core idea of the so-called altered law compatibilism (ALC).[46]

In a similar vein, the so-called altered past compatibilism (APC) maintains, no less surprisingly at first view, that the distant past is, in a sense to be qualified carefully of course, up to us. I will focus on ALC, though, in order to save space, and the law issue will turn out to be pertinent with respect to other components of Kant's overall position with regard to a guarantee of perpetual peace.

The key elements in Kant's solution are the following (see CPR A532–A537/ B560–B565): In order to safeguard freedom strong enough to sustain morality we need to be able to uphold transcendental freedom, the ability to bring about a state of affairs spontaneously – and this in the face of the determinism holding in the world or realm of appearances established through the means of theoretical philosophy (whatever these may be precisely). For Kant, this kind of freedom is only feasible when the bearer of this freedom is located in the realm of things in themselves (remember this distinction is mentioned by Kant in the guarantor footnote) and the effects of this freedom occur in the realm of appearances. This claim is of course not without its own problems, but my aim here is to sketch Kant's solution rather than to defend it.

Since freedom, in some sense at least, is something like a causal power, and every efficient cause needs to have a character, there must be something like an intelligible character of the noumenal agent or agent as a thing in itself, just as the agent as a natural cause must have an empirical character. A character of a cause, in this sense of the term "character" at least, is for Kant a law of its causality (CPR A538f./B A566f.).

In the first *Critique* (CPR A556/B584), this intelligible character is something like a contingent feature of each of these agents; their respective intelligible characters could have been different. Moreover, for Kant, it is not caused by anything external to this agent, but is due to the will of the individual agent. In the second *Critique* (5: 98) and in the *Religion* (6: 27, 31f.) Kant expands upon this idea and maintains that these intelligible characters have been acquired by the noumenal agents themselves.

In addition to this, in case of human free agency there is a counterfactual dependency of the empirical character of the agent on its intelligible character. A different intelligible character would have resulted in a different empirical character (CPR A556/B584). Finally, the empirical character is a sign or effect of the intelligible character for Kant (CPR A546/B574). In short, for Kant, in

---

[46] See Ertl (1998: 238–249, 2004, 2014), Vilhauer (2004), Pereboom (2006) and Watkins (2005: 329–339) for more detailed accounts of Kant's position in terms of ALC. Rosefeldt (2012) discusses this strategy in depth as well as the related account of Kant in terms of altered past compatibilism.

case of free agents their empirical characters are derivative from their intelligible characters.

We are thus beginning to see how this strategy can aim at undermining premise (ii) in the consequence argument. In summary, at least some of the laws of nature are up to us insofar as our intelligible characters are up to us. Since the empirical character provides the special laws of nature required for a naturalist explanation of the effects of the free action in the realm of appearances (in turn indispensable for Kant's methodological naturalism), the laws in question reflect the intelligible character; a different intelligible character could and indeed would bring about a difference in the special laws of nature, and since the intelligible character is due to the individual free agent, some of the special laws of nature can also be said to be due to this free agent.

According to this reading, the noumenal free agent makes a difference in the realm of appearances by influencing what the special laws of nature are, which in turn make up its form, as I said above.

Let us now look at the notion of an intelligible character more closely. What exactly is this intelligible character? How can we understand it? What is its status? In particular, how is acquisition of it supposed to work, how counterfactual dependency? Here, we can seek help from what looks like an unlikely source, but one which fits perfectly well with the dogmatic tone of the footnote.

As I said, passages in the guarantee addendum and, in particular, in the guarantee footnote sound as if they belong to the kind of dogmatic metaphysics overcome in and through Kant's critical turn. They are best read as spelling out what, exactly, we commit ourselves to when accepting or assuming the existence and the pertinent concept of God on practical grounds. This includes how these commitments can be rendered coherent with the results of the transcendental approach to the sphere of space and time – for example, its objects being subjected to causal laws. Assuming the existence of God in accordance with the concept of him sustained by the moral argument requires the assumption of the real possibility of God, and it requires assuming the logical possibility that this real possibility coexists with the real possibility pertinent to the realm of appearances and the conditions of the possibility of experience. Put somewhat differently, we have to spell out how an entity with all the attributes ascribed to it from practical considerations can 'coexist' with the transcendental 'machinery' argued for mainly in the transcendental analytic.

Similarly, the claims about an intelligible character are best viewed as conceptual implications of the assumption of transcendental freedom. As indicated above, we might wish to call this the libertarian, or asymmetrically libertarian, element of Kant's practically grounded metaphysics as opposed to its theist part. Both lie beyond the realms of genuine knowledge, since we do not have a corresponding intuition which would be required to complement the conceptual claims.

For the sake of its internal consistency, this libertarian part also needs to be compatible both with the other parts of the practically grounded metaphysics and with the transcendental account of the realm of appearances. It must be logically possible that both natural determinism and transcendental freedom and, along with it, the intelligible characters are both actual and hence both *realiter* possible, each in its own way.[47] If we have reasons to assume the actuality of transcendental freedom, as we must by virtue of morality, we must assume the actuality and hence real possibility of an intelligible character, although we cannot know how real possibility can be accounted for in the realm of things in themselves.

Finally, the theist part and the libertarian part need to fit together, but investigating this concerns the other facets of the problem of human freedom which we will consider in more detail below. This theist part, as we shall see in a moment, is at least to some extent also used by Kant to illustrate the compatibility of human freedom with his transcendental account of the world in space and time.

3.3 Intelligible Characters and Counterfactuals of Freedom

The notion of the intelligible character is a contentious issue in Kant scholarship. One way of making sense of it is to draw on an idea developed in the early modern debates about human freedom,[48] that is, in an environment where many of the key concepts discussed and transformed by Kant, such as "providence" and *concursus*, were developed and investigated. This is the idea of what

---

[47] See Ludwig (2015) for an important discussion of these problems. Ludwig criticizes what he calls the "standard interpretation" of mistakenly focusing on the *logical* possibility of transcendental freedom and instead takes Kant to have established its *real* possibility in the resolution to the third antinomy.

[48] This is the debate, embedded in a much more comprehensive controversy about *concursus*, providence and grace (the very concepts dealt with in the guarantor footnote), between the Molinists and the Thomists triggered by the publication of Molina's *Concordia* in 1585. See Freddoso (1988a: 1–8, 36–42) and MacGregor (2015: 79–105) for details. The main disagreement about counterfactuals of freedom concerned the question as to whether they are pre-volitional or post-volitional with regard to God's will, that is, whether God has control over their truth-value. The Molinists denied, while the Thomists endorsed, divine control. My attempt at reading Kant's conception of the intelligible characters in terms of cfs is neutral to this controversy, while Kant's doctrine of the self-acquisition of the intelligible characters by the human free agents themselves, in my opinion, suggests an affinity to Molina's position. As we shall see further below, there are further striking parallels between Kant's doctrines relating to grace and providence and those put forward by Molina. For a detailed account of Molina's impact on a number of early modern philosophers see Piro (2014), and for a more comprehensive take on Molina's importance for Kant's peculiar form of compatibilism, namely, his "libertarian compatibilism," see Ertl (2014) and the discussion in Rosefeldt (2012) and Hogan (2014).

nowadays is called a "counterfactual of freedom."[49] By virtue of the epistemological qualifications just reiterated, this is not, of course, to suggest that Kant regards or is committed to regarding this doctrine as a theoretical truth and the object of human knowledge. Rather, this idea is a conceptual commitment in the wake of our endorsement of transcendental freedom which hinges on the validity of the categorical imperative.

In addition to this, the idea in question had originally been devised within theories meant to reconcile the compatibility of divine knowledge and human freedom, that is, the foreknowledge facet (2) from our list in the introduction to this section. Within these debates, one particularly important question concerned the truth of propositions about how free agents *would* behave in certain circumstances, and the divine knowledge of these propositions in the so-called *scientia media*.[50] As we shall see, however, the idea in question is sufficiently rich to be applicable to other facets of this problem as well; most importantly, to the issues pertinent in facet (4), the natural causal facet of the problem of freedom.

One plausible way of reading Kant's conception of the intelligible character is indeed to take an intelligible character of a free agent to consist of all the true counterfactuals of freedom valid for this free agent. The structure of a counterfactual of freedom ("cf") is as follows: If person P were in situation S, they would freely perform action A. We may call "P were in Situation S" the antecedent ("a") and "P would freely perform A" the consequent ("c"). Rendering the structure of a cf in a more formal way, it would be something like $a \square \rightarrow c$. In some accounts of cfs in the literature, both in a and c, a specific point in time is indicated ("at t"),[51] and there are restrictions as to what is feasible as a proper account or specification of a situation. Crucially, this framework allows us to distinguish what the agent could do in the specified situation and what the agent would do. Moreover, this framework allows us to maintain that instead of what the agent would do, the agent could do something else, so that what the agent would do is up to the agent.

Two main arguments support the identification of the intelligible character of a noumenal agent with the counterfactuals of freedom true of this agent. First,

---

[49] For further details see Trinkaus Zagzebski (1991: 125–152); Perszyk (2011a); Dekker (2000); Hasker, Basinger and Dekker (2000); Perszyk (2011b). The most concise account is still Freddoso (1988a).

[50] *Scientia media* is supposed to be midway between *scientia naturalis* of what is necessary (which includes what is necessarily possible) and *scientia visionis* of what is actual. To be sure, the controversy about *scientia media* and counterfactuals of freedom concerns only one part of facet (1). God's knowledge of what *will* happen in the future and its compatibility with human freedom is of course at least equally important, albeit not for our purposes. For a comprehensive discussion of facet (1) see Fischer (1989) and Hogan (2014).

[51] See, for example, Wierenga (2011: 118).

the identification coheres well with the definition of "intelligible character" in terms of a law of causality, since it is precisely the function of a law to provide the information about how the agent would act in all possible circumstances. Second, a recently proposed principle which elucidates how there can be true counterfactuals of freedom can provide an account of the acquisition of the intelligible character. This principle, usually called GP+ or the "extended grounding principle," says:

> Any true contingent proposition is true in virtue of some concrete state of affairs that does exist, or has existed, or will exist, *or would exist (under specified conditions)*. (Flint 2011: 39, emphasis mine)[52]

In the literature on Kant, there are basically two types of accounts as to how, for him, the intelligible character is acquired. According to the first conception, the acquisition comes about in a timeless one-off action reminiscent of the motive of a choice of a form of life in Plato's *Republic*.[53] According to the second conception, such an acquisition is to be construed in terms of the sum total of the agent's actions, or in terms of a function of a number of more conventional individual free actions of an agent, such as telling a lie.[54] It has been suggested recently that these actions are all the actual past, present and future conventional free actions of an agent. My reading can strengthen the second conception in several important respects and retain its main advantage of what we can call a little-by-little account of character acquisition in terms of conventional free actions. What I propose in line with the idea underlying GP+ is to construe this acquisition precisely in terms of all the actions an agent *would* freely carry out in all possible situations. Since these hypothetical actions are actions of each individual will and are not necessitated by anything external (nor internal) to the individual will, the character consisting of all the cfs may indeed be said to be acquired by the agent. In this manner, the agent herself in and through these hypothetical actions adds a set of truths about herself to the set of truths which hold about that agent but over which the agent has no control.

The hypothetical free actions are those by virtue of which the consequents of the cfs are true. This means that individual actions account for the generality of the law which makes up the intelligible character; this law cannot be used as an explanation of these actions and is therefore not a law of nature. Seen this way, the account given so far also covers facet (5) of the problem of freedom: it is not the case that the presence of any truthmaker threatens freedom. The presence of those truthmakers does not do so which are due to the human

---

[52] Responding to Hasker (2011).

[53] This suggestion has been put forward by Wood (1984: 89–93).

[54] This account has been developed by Willaschek (1992: 149–167) and put forward again, in a modified form, by McCarty (2009: 148–154).

will. In the account suggested, it is therefore *not* the case that the truth of the consequents in the cfs preempts what the agent would do in the situation specified in the antecedent. Rather, the action in question is the truthmaker,[55] and this, again, is consistent with the agent being able to act otherwise and the action being up the agent.

Of course, the intelligible character cannot be *known* by a human observer, but this does not speak against this conception, since truth and knowledge about it can be separate in Kant, at least as far as the realm of things in themselves is concerned. Still, somebody who could know how each individual agent would act in each possible situation has important knowledge about that agent. Arguably, anybody who claims to know the *Gesinnung* or fundamental attitude of an agent would need to know the intelligible character as understood in this manner.

Indeed, insofar as Kant speaks of God as the scrutinizer of the heart who does know the *Gesinnung* of each agent (e.g., Rel 6: 99), and insofar as Kant assumes that knowledge of *Gesinnung* presupposes knowledge of what an agent would do in (sometimes challenging) situations (see MM 6: 392–393) which do not need to become actual, Kant ascribes such knowledge to God.

In this manner and understood in this way, the notion of the intelligible character fits in well into Kant's take on the multifaceted problem of human freedom and indicates that the original point of the early modern debate, namely, that we should take counterfactuals of freedom to be the object of a special form of divine knowledge, is still detectable in Kant.

We should therefore not be distracted by the fact that in the lectures on natural theology Kant dismisses *scientia media* as a useless distinction (PhilTh-P 28: 1055), since what he dismisses under this heading has almost nothing to do with the early modern conception of it. Kant's talk of God as knowing the *Gesinnung* of an agent is indicative that, implicitly at least, Kant concedes something like middle knowledge as originally conceived. Nonetheless, attributing such a type of knowledge to God is again a doctrine pertaining to practically grounded metaphysics, not something we are licensed to claim as a theoretical truth.

With this settled we can move on. The counterfactual dependency or, more broadly, the derivative status of the empirical character, and hence of the special laws of nature with regard to the intelligible character, can be elucidated further in terms of Kant's doctrine of the regulative use of reason. For example, he maintains in Rel 6: 142 that God needs to be regarded as the origin of laws of nature, and in CPR A694–A697/B722–B725 that within the regulative use of

---

[55] One might, perhaps, think that the uncausedness of the will with regard to this action disqualifies it as a truthmaker, but this claim simply presupposes that a truthmaker needs to be caused. At any rate, its uncausedness is different from its role as a truthmaker.

reason we need to regard the systematic unity of the world and of the laws describing it as originating in God's creative intellect. Passages in the CJ, such as 5: 180, point in similar directions, and there Kant even focuses on "particular empirical laws." To be sure, the mode in which these claims can be made is not that of knowledge.

These passages indicate that for Kant the special laws of nature are due to the divine intellect, but this does not tell us why the laws are as they are. With regard to this question we get some hints in the "Doctrine of Method" section of the first *Critique*; these are passages which *explicitly* support the idea of God as that in virtue of which nature and freedom coincide. Kant now focuses on the divine will, which is, of course, pertinent for the implementation of laws:

> This will must be omnipotent, so that all of nature and its relation to morality in the world are subject to it; omniscient so that it cognizes the inmost dispositions and their moral worth; omnipresent, so that it is immediately ready for every need that is demanded by the highest good for the world; eternal, so that this agreement of nature and freedom is not lacking at any time, etc. (CPR A815/B843)

These passages suggest that we need to include a special predicate in the concept of a divine will in order to secure the agreement of nature and freedom. One way of illustrating how this agreement can be achieved is to assume that special natural laws are enacted which somehow reflect the intelligible characters. In order to be in a position to do this, the will in question must be eternal, that is, beyond time.

Kant offers a more detailed account when bringing together the libertarian and the theist lines of his practically grounded metaphysics in the lectures on natural theology, expanding upon the hints he gives in the critical works themselves. What he says there points exactly in the direction just mentioned. These lectures, of course, are not on the same footing as Kant's published works.[56] However, and as we shall see, what he is said to have laid out in these lectures complies exactly with what he is logically committed to by virtue of the interconnection of positions possible with regard to each facet of the problem of freedom.

In a sense the lectures are, at least in principle, appropriate to consult for our purposes since there we find a more comprehensive treatment of his practically grounded metaphysics; they are in this respect rather close to what he is doing in the guarantor footnote.

Strikingly, in his lectures on natural theology, Kant accounts for the derivative status of the special laws of nature in terms of his conception of providence.

---

[56] See Clewis (2015) for a comprehensive take on the issue of what to make of Kant's lectures.

As indicated in section 2, in the Pölitz lectures, Kant is reported to have defined "providence" as follows:

> Divine *providence* consists in the institution of the laws according to which the course of the world is to proceed. (PhilTh-P 28: 1110)

Crucially, he is reported to have added an important detail:

> For certainly in his omniscience he [i.e., God] foresaw every possible individual, as well as every *genus*, even before there was anything at all. And in actualizing them he provided for their existence as well as their welfare, through the establishment of suitable laws. (PhilTh-P 28: 1111)

This passage can plausibly be read as indicating that the counterfactual dependency of the special laws of nature on the respective intelligible characters is based on divine knowledge of these individuals prior to the creation and the subsequent implementation of the appropriate special laws of nature. Had the characters been different, the special laws of nature would have been different, because different laws of nature would have been implemented.[57]

Clearly, some of the events Kant talks about in this passage must be (aspects of) human actions and, as he emphasizes a little later in the text, it must be in a human being's power whether to observe or disobey the laws of morality, even though the choice of disobedience would be counter to the divine plan with regard to the moral world.[58]

This rather more detailed and certainly less abstract account of ALC blends in nicely with a key result obtained in section 2, namely, the identification of nature in a formal sense and providence in the object sense when regarded from the perspective of the unity of theoretical and practical reason. What we have now is the addition of the idea that this formal aspect of nature reflects, or is at least in part due to, human freedom. In this manner, we can also make some sense of the idea expressed in one of the key sentences of the guarantor footnote that this

---

[57] In this regard, if God has no control over the intelligible characters, Kant's account of providence is, at least in this respect, similar to Molina's for which human free acts can only be fitted into providential oversight, and are not determined by the divine will. See Flint (1998) again for a comprehensive take on Molina's doctrine of providence, and Flint (2009) for a succinct account of all the standard conceptions of providence, namely, the Thomist, open theist and Molinist ones.

[58] To be sure, the primacy of these events with regard to the laws that make up the intelligible characters does not turn Kant into a Humean with regard to his overall conception of natural laws. Rather, the special laws of nature are integrated into a system of laws with metaphysical and ultimately transcendental principles of conservation, causality and interaction as its foundation. Thus, these special laws can underwrite causal necessity, whereas they are not metaphysically necessary, that is, valid in every possible world. For an attempt to show how some of the special laws of nature can be integrated into a system of laws with regard to such a system combining, indeed balancing out, a priori and a posteriori elements see Friedman (1992). For a succinct account of the unity and diversity of laws in Kant see Watkins (2017).

form of nature has been "determined beforehand" by the world author, and we can see now that determination is at least in one important respect epistemic insofar as this form must be in accordance with the intelligible characters of the human agents. The determining is at the same time constitutive since according to this view the laws are implemented through the divine will.

But what are special natural laws which reflect the intelligible characters? Along the lines of the reading of the intelligible character suggested, one minimal condition could be as follows: The special laws of nature must be such that they sustain counterfactuals about the agents taken as appearances – "counterfactuals of nature," as we could call them – with the same antecedents and consequents[59] as in the counterfactuals of freedom. The difference between a counterfactual of freedom and a corresponding counterfactual of nature would then be that, when taking the special laws of nature as fixed, it is not up to the agent – when regarded as an appearance – how to act in the situation described in the antecedent. In this vein, it is what has been called the "order of nature" itself, which turns out to be at least in part due to human freedom; within this order of nature the mechanism of nature can do its work.

3.4 Multifaceted Compatibility

As shown above, there are at least five different facets of the problem of freedom that are relevant for Kant and detectable in the guarantee addendum, each corresponding to a doctrine which threatens to undermine human freedom, namely: (1) the facet of divine foreknowledge; (2) the facet of creation or ontological dependency; (3) the concurrentist facet; (4) the facet of natural causal determinism; and (5) the truth theoretical facet.

While the natural causal facet (4) of the problem of freedom is clearly the most pressing and important one, the other four are situated more on the periphery, especially as far as scholarly discussion is concerned. Nonetheless, the solutions Kant proposes for each of these facets are in an important sense interconnected, since positions with regard to the foreknowledge facet (1) have implications for those with regard to the natural causal facet (4) and the truth theoretical facet (5), while positions taken with regard to the creation facet (2) have, in turn, implications for those with regard to the other three. If Kant were to explain divine knowledge about human free agency in terms of God's bringing about truths relating to the intelligible characters, it is difficult to see how he could maintain that the intelligible characters are self-procured by the individual agents. Similarly, if Kant were to maintain that through creation God fixes the truth values of the cfs that make up the intelligible characters, how could these truth values still be regarded as being due to the agents themselves?

---

[59] Except, of course, for the adverb "freely."

Conversely, such a position with regard to creation would fit well with an explanation of divine knowledge of these truths by virtue of some kind of maker's knowledge in respect of the intelligible characters, as we might wish to put it.

Indeed, with regard to facet (2), the pertinent passages in the second *Critique* (5: 100–102) and the *Religion* (6: 142–143) all suggest, or make sense on, the assumption that there are no options on the part of God with regard to the human free agents he can create, in the sense that it is beyond his control how they use their freedom, that is, which intelligible character they acquire. In the *Religion*, Kant goes even as far as to say that we need to represent the free agents as if they preexisted and thus as exempted from the creation thesis for the sake of their freedom. True, this claim seems to contrast with Kant's mere conservationism, expressed in the example of the physician and his remedies in the guarantor footnote (TPP 8: 361.39–362.32fn) and discussed above in section 2. Recall that Kant clearly says that if one wishes to ascend to the *Urgrund* or first ground of all things, the physician and his remedies need to be regarded as created and God, in turn, regarded as the sufficient cause for the recovery of the patient in question. Strikingly, in the example, Kant completely abstracts from the question of free agency and treats the actions of the physician merely as natural events. In this vein, Kant can be read as maintaining that when taking the recovery of a patient as the effect of natural causes, we can – in the framework provided by his practically grounded metaphysics – alternatively regard it as the indirect effect of divine creative activity, although, and this must be stressed, this would not amount to a proper explanation for Kant.

This reading does not by itself commit us to saying that for Kant the same is true when regarding the recovery of the patient as the effect of a free action by the physician (regarded as a thing in itself). Plainly, when taking the physician as a free agent, we cannot fully ascribe the action to God. Moreover, the passage in the *Religion* insists that, for the sake of freedom, we even need to *represent* the free agent as preexisting and exempt from divine creative activity, since otherwise we would have to take the alleged free cause to be configured by the creator. Accordingly, Kant's emphasis really seems to be on maintaining that the intelligible characters of agents are something pregiven even to God and that he has no choice about which free agents can be rendered actual. Accordingly, with regard to facet (1), God's grasp of these intelligible characters should be taken as tracking truths rather than bringing them about.[60]

---

[60] According to Perszyk (2011a) and Piro (2014), maintaining that there are pre-volitional counterfactuals of freedom and that God has knowledge of them amounts to Molinism in a minimal sense.

By virtue of this relation of the facets described so far, Kant can be read as trying to avoid positions which endanger the self-procured status of the intelligible character (which, in turn, is the key claim of his libertarian compatibilism).

Facet (3) might be approached by considering a similar idea at work here too, but this of course would require far more detailed enquires than are possible here. Suffice it to say that Kant's surprising statement about the indispensability of the notion of *concursus* with regard to grace in the guarantee footnote is consistent with him distinguishing, implicitly at least, what has been called prevenient and justificatory grace.[61] While in the second piece of the *Religion* Kant is evidently and primarily concerned with justificatory grace and the problem of something like a divine "pardon." The passage in the guarantee footnote, by contrast, can be read as having to do with prevenient grace. Moreover, what Kant says is consistent with the idea that justificatory grace presupposes the effect of prevenient grace (for reaching a state of mind – in this case, faith – indispensable for pardon) and that the coming about of this effect, in turn, presupposes human cooperation which is beyond God's control.[62]

Facet (3) is important because it touches upon the ultimate end of the world author. As we have seen in section 2, this end is concerned with the moralization of human agents and the suggestion in the pertinent section of the guarantee footnote seems to be, rather surprisingly, that grace, and along with it concurrentism, is indispensable for this.

Provided that my brief sketch of Kant's strategy for tackling the problems related to facet (3) is correct, a common feature of his position with regard to all the five facets of the problem of human freedom emerges. For Kant, there seems to be some sort of priority of human free agency, even in its hypothetical employment, with respect to which nature, truth and, in certain respects at least, even some features of God himself are derivative. This is perhaps particularly striking with regard to God's knowledge of the *intelligible characters* of the free agents, and in the next section I shall provide further, more direct evidence for such a reading. Along the lines I am suggesting, this knowledge should be regarded as truth tracking and hence as limiting the options of what he can do. Understood in this manner, God cannot make it the case that – as we need to put it in the parlance of cfs – an agent would act differently from how they would in fact act in a certain situation. Similarly, according to my account

---

[61] See, for example, Pasternack (2014: 168fn8) and Muchnik and Pasternack (2017: 263fn7).

[62] This reading of Kant's position on grace indicates a further parallel to Molina, who famously endorsed such a view. As far as I can see, this parallel has so far remained undetected in the increasingly intense debate about Kant on grace. For an overview of Molina's position see MacGregor (2015: 60–73); for Kant see Duplá (2016) as well as Muchnik and Pasternack (2017).

of facet (3), God cannot even 'force' human agents into moral goodness through grace, since even in this regard God needs to rely on human cooperation.

To be sure, emphasizing the priority of freedom makes it more difficult to establish both the compatibility thesis, with regard to each and all the different facets of the problem of freedom, and the guarantee thesis as well, so I take it that this point can be granted for the purpose of my argument even though it merits a more comprehensive treatment.

While, when seen in the manner suggested, the options of divine agency are restricted by virtue of human freedom, the situation with regard to knowledge is nonetheless markedly different, and this is precisely because of the knowledge regarding the intelligible characters. This suggests that the way open to a God conceived of in terms of a practically grounded metaphysics for succeeding in obtaining the actions wanted from a free agent is for God to bring the agent into a situation in which God knows the agent would freely act in this way.

Arguably, this way of handling free agents is in the widest possible sense political – political in the realm of metaphysics even – but the problem is that, given Kant's very stance on the priority of human freedom, it is not a matter of course that these free human agents would ever act in the way they should. Put differently, it is not obvious why the intelligible characters are such that they lead to special laws of nature which play their part in securing perpetual peace.

4 Freedom and the Guarantee

We have seen in section 2 how the guarantor powers are related and in section 3 how the 'activity' or 'presence' of the guarantor powers is consistent with human freedom. This still leaves the third question open, namely, why, for Kant, there is such a guarantee of perpetual peace in the first place, and why he thinks he can be sure that events are channeled toward perpetual peace or that history is converging on perpetual peace.

In order to answer this question, we need to stay in the mode of discourse of a practically grounded metaphysics a bit longer, rather than shun or ignore the passages in the guarantee addendum where it is pertinent.

To recap, while Kant engages in this discourse in the guarantee addendum, he takes the problem of freedom in all its multifaceted dimensions as solved. As pointed out in section 3, further textual material of this kind, especially from the lectures on natural theology, can help us to understand Kant's multifaceted compatibility claim. In this final section, I will try to show how Kant can justify the guarantee claim despite his commitment to the priority of human freedom, which would seem to put even more pressure on the guarantee thesis. In fact,

Kant's strategy in tackling the compatibility problem will turn out to provide the key to the justification of the guarantee thesis.

I will look first at the issue of the objective ultimate end of creation again, which consists in the fulfillment of a duty for human agents by human agents. I shall establish, on Kant's behalf, why there is a guarantee for the achievement of this ultimate end. Subsequently, the 'mode of operation' of the pertinent guarantor device shall be sketched briefly. Finally, the reasons for the guarantee thesis with regard to perpetual peace will be investigated by determining the relationship of perpetual peace to the ultimate end.

4.1 The Guarantee of the Objective Ultimate End

Let us now examine why for Kant the coming about of the objective ultimate end of creation is certain. It must be said, though, that Kant does not state this point explicitly, but it follows from a number of key assumptions he makes.[63] In order to see why this is the case, we need to look at the extraordinary sentence from the main text of the guarantor addendum again.

> That which provides this liability (guarantee) is nothing less than the great artist nature (*natura daedala rerum*) in whose mechanical course purposiveness visibly shines forth, to let unity come up through the disunity of men even against their will, and [which] is therefore called fate like a compulsion through a cause unbeknownst to us with regard to its laws of efficacy, and when considering its purposefulness in the course of the world, as a deep-lying wisdom of a higher cause directed to the objective ultimate end of the human species and predetermining this course of the world, called providence, which strictly speaking we do not know from the institutions of art in nature and cannot even infer from them but (as in all relations of the form of things to ends as such) we can and must add in thinking, in order to have a concept of its possibility in analogy to human actions of art, but to imagine the relation of it and consonance to the end (the moral one) immediately prescribed by reason is an idea which is effusive in a theoretical respect, but which in a practical respect (for example, with regard to the concept of the duty of perpetual peace, in order to use that mechanism of nature for it) is dogmatic and well grounded concerning its reality. (TPP 8: 360.12–362.11, my translation)

What Kant is saying in the latter half of this passage is this: When it comes to the consonance of providence with the moral end immediately prescribed by reason we transcend the realm of theory, but we are entitled to claim this from

---

[63] In the strategy of drawing on Kant's conception of the ultimate end of creation for establishing the guarantee thesis with regard to perpetual peace I am following Mertens (1995), but Mertens appears to read this thesis in a moderate form, short of the future actuality thesis.

a practical perspective. In section 2, it was argued that this end is the free acquisition of a good will by at least some of the human agents.

In the guarantor footnote, the form of nature – which, as argued above, from the standpoint of unified reason is identical to providence in the object sense – is explicitly connected to the "end of a world author" by Kant. I said above that I take this end to be the "objective ultimate end," but as we shall see, the argument works just as well with ends subordinate to it. Let us look at the relevant passage again:

> In the mechanism of nature to which the human being also belongs (as a sense entity), a form manifests itself which already lies at the ground of its existence and which we cannot render comprehensible other than by putting the end of a world author underneath it who determines it beforehand . . . (TPP 8: 361.5– 8fn, my translation)

The question is: Where could the certainty with regard to achieving this end come from? According to Kant, and as explained above, the moral argument not only provides grounds for accepting the existence of God, but a determinate concept of God as well. In the intension of this concept, as set out in CPR A815/ B843 for example, we find traditional predicates such as omnipotence and omniscience. An enquiry into the precise conception of these predicates would lead too far here, but given the results in section 3 concerning Kant's altered law compatibilism the alternatives can be stated quite boldly.

We have seen that, for Kant, the intelligible characters of agents ground at least some of the special laws of nature. One way of arguing for the certainty of the achievement of the ultimate objective end would be to say that, due to his omnipotence, God can simply configure or arrange the intelligible characters of the human agents in such a way that they lead to special laws of nature which, together with the material conditions provided by nature, lead to a course of events culminating in the actualization of the ultimate objective end. This very broad sketch would of course be in need of many more details and a great number of qualifications (in particular, since a good will is not something belonging to the realm of appearances), but the overall direction of the argument is perfectly clear.

While this line of reasoning coheres with not altogether unproblematic claims made in the secondary literature[64] according to which for the critical Kant – with all the qualifications which are required for such a claim pertaining to a practically grounded metaphysics – God *necessarily* creates the best possible world, I take this thesis not to be compatible with Kant's ideas about the priority and bedrock status of human freedom. To be sure, should it be possible to uphold the priority

---

[64] See the discussion in Insole (2013: 16–24).

and bedrock status of human freedom within this approach, it would be much easier to establish certainty with regard to the coming about of the objective ultimate end.

The difficult route to establishing this certainty starts from the assumption that the priority and bedrock status of human freedom implies that the intelligible characters are pregiven even to God, and limit his options of what world to create (with the latter again taken as a doctrine of practically grounded metaphysics, of course).

There is a further passage from the lectures on natural theology which supports this assumption and at the same time provides the resources for resolving the difficulties that arise along with it. To reiterate, these lectures are not on the same footing as Kant's published works. Nonetheless, the passage in question fits much better with the priority and bedrock status idea Kant is committed to by virtue of the multifaceted compatibility claim he makes. This position, as has been shown in section 3, commits him to the idea that the intelligible characters are self-acquired by the noumenal agents rather than assigned to them by somebody else. In the passage in question Kant says:

> God's infinite understanding, on the contrary, recognized the *possibility of a highest good* external to himself in which morality would be the supreme principle. He was conscious at the same time of having all the power needed to set up this most perfect of all possible worlds. His well-pleasedness in this consciousness of himself as an all-sufficient ground was therefore the only thing determining his will to actualize the greatest finite good. (PhilTh-P 28: 1102)

This passage is remarkable in a number of respects. First of all, there is a clear distinction between the possibility of an external highest good and the capacity to "set [it] up." Obviously then, this capacity is not a matter of course. This suggests that – again, as an assumption justified in practically grounded meta-physics – God realized or grasped that the intelligible characters, self-acquired by the noumenal agents, are conducive to this end. It is precisely this emphasis on the epistemic perfection of the divine intellect which accords well with the idea of the truth-tracking function of it with regard to the intelligible characters.

In this vein, there is no further reason as to why the intelligible characters are conducive to the actualization of the highest good. Rather, this has to count as the perhaps ultimate contingency.[65] Given that God must be regarded as having created the world as a rational agent and hence on the basis of knowledge of the intelligible characters, practically grounded metaphysics licenses the

---

[65] Against this background, we can finally address the deeper reason for Kant's puzzling inclusion of "fate" (*Schicksal*) among the labels for the guarantor power of perpetual peace (TPP 8: 361.1). The fate aspect plausibly has its application here since there is no further account possible of this ultimate contingency.

assumption that he knew what would happen if he contributed his part in actualizing the world and, even more specifically, that he knew that in this case the objective ultimate end would become actual. We are even told that having the capacity to set up the best possible world was the reason for embarking upon the creative enterprise in the first place. As long as we assume the existence of God as specified in the concept developed so far, and since knowledge implies truth, we can therefore conclude that, since God did contribute his part in actualizing this world, the objective ultimate end will become actual.

While, in this approach based on practically grounded metaphysics, there is no further reason as to why the intelligible characters should be conducive to the actualization of the highest good, the very existence of the world is *indicative* that this is in fact the case. It is knowledge which compensates for the lack of control over the intelligible characters on the part of the God of Kant's practically grounded metaphysics. Hence, delegating the actualization of the highest good to human free agents does not undercut the certainty of it coming about; the point is rather that one must acknowledge that this certainty is not a matter of metaphysical necessity.

4.2 The Path toward the Objective Ultimate End

Once it has been established that the intelligible characters of the human agents are conducive to the overall point of bringing about a world in the first place, we can see how delegating the actualization of this goal works on the basis of knowing these characters. William Lane Craig has illustrated this with regard to counterfactuals of freedom, in terms of which – as I have argued in section 3 – Kant's notion of the intelligible character can be accounted for.

> Since God knows what any free creature would do in any situation, he can, by creating the appropriate situations, bring it about that creatures will achieve his ends and purposes and that they will do so *freely*. When one considers that these situations are themselves the results of earlier free decisions by creatures, free decisions which God had to bring about, one begins to see that providence over a world of free creatures could only be the work of omniscience. Only an infinite Mind could calculate the unimaginably complex and numerous factors that would need to be combined in order to bring about through the free decisions of creatures a single human event such as, say, the enactment of the lend-lease policy prior to America's entry into the Second World War. Think then of God's planning the entire course of world history so as to achieve his purposes! Given middle knowledge, the apparent contradiction between God's sovereignty, which seems to crush human freedom, and human freedom, which seems to break God's sovereignty, is resolved. In his infinite intelligence, God is able to plan a world in which his designs are achieved by creatures acting freely. (Craig 1987: 135, in Trinkaus Zagzebski 1991:128)

To every reader of Kant's essay on *Perpetual Peace*, Craig's account sounds perfectly familiar, since what we have in Kant's text is the idea of a similar guarantor device for the end in question. Seen retrospectively, the historical development can be interpreted as having occurred in such a way that human agents made the suitable decisions to initiate a process toward the objective ultimate end of creation.[66] Of course, and to repeat, perpetual peace is not the objective ultimate end, and we will get back to this issue again below, but at any rate the contours of how Kant's guarantor claim can be rendered intelligible are beginning to take shape.

We have seen above that, in Kant, from the perspective of unified reason, nature in the formal sense of the term can be identified with providence in the object sense of the term. Moreover, in Kant, it is nature which also takes the role of setting the required conditions for starting and upholding the historical process, as his employment of the *theatrum mundi* metaphor suggests.

> Before we determine this guarantee in more detail, it will be necessary to examine the state which nature has organized for the persons acting on her grand stage and which finally renders necessary its securing of peace, and then the way in which it does this. (TPP 8: 362f., my translation)

In the guarantee addendum (TPP 8: 365–368) we not only find the idea of something like a first set of conditions, but of an iterated or ongoing development of sets of conditions which in this text are described in legal and political terms. This mainly concerns the emerging imperfect legal systems which are, partially at least, the result of human action. Similarly, the transfer to a republican system in the as yet imperfect individual states, occurring through self-interest (against the background of a still unfettered propensity toward evil at the level of mature beings), brings about a new set of conditions. The same idea is present in the claim of a *prevention* of a certain possible development in that by means of the emergence of different languages and religions the establishment of a universal monarchy will be undercut. A universal monarchy would be an institutional setting unfit for perpetual peace (because of its ultimate collapse into anarchy and hence the destruction of even an imperfect legal order). Again, similarly and partially overlapping with the development of the conditions reached so far in the individual states, the emerging spirit of trade leads to a significant shift with regard to actions regarding their external relations, namely, according to Kant, to a gradual cessation of war.[67]

---

[66] See Anderson-Gold (2012) for a detailed account of the importance of an interpretive stance on history for providing orientation for progress.

[67] For a more comprehensive account of the trajectory toward perpetual peace both as the destination of the natural history of man and the ultimate end of the doctrine of right, involving human beings as merely rational beings, as rational beings equipped with pure practical reason and as

Abstracting from the at times bewildering details we are confronted with, the general structure of Kant's account is quite clearly detectable: There was a set of antecedent conditions provided by nature in the sense that it was the result of events involving no specifically human contribution. Against the background of these antecedent conditions and owing to the mechanism of nature, humans – insofar as they are part of nature – performed actions which led to renewed antecedent conditions in which again certain actions occurred, the results of which, in sum, can in turn count as "stepping-stone(s)"[68] toward the objective ultimate end of creation.

In light of these considerations, key points raised in section 2 can finally be clarified, albeit again with regard to the objective ultimate end first. In this section, I indicated that neither the reflective usage reading nor the technical-practical reading of Kant's doctrine of a usage of the mechanism of nature for something which is a moral duty to be brought about can fully capture what Kant is aiming at. It is now relatively straightforward to see, against the background of a practically grounded metaphysics consonant with the findings of the transcendental account of the realm of space and time, that the subject of this 'usage' must be none other than the world author. This does not, of course, rule out that political agents should aim at something similar, nor that the idea of such a usage can help us come to terms with the philosophical problem of perpetual peace, but what we can call the "providence reading" of this doctrine occupies the focal position, at least in the guarantee addendum.

In a similar vein, it is now possible to elucidate Kant's – on the first view – perplexing claims about nature as the guarantor power. On the one hand, Kant maintains that from a theoretical standpoint the term "nature" is appropriate out of epistemic modesty, while also insisting that the theoretical standpoint cannot provide the means for underwriting the guarantee thesis in the sense that the end in question will become actual. Still, Kant is endorsing such a future actuality reading nonetheless. We can read Kant in the following manner here: The guarantee in this strong sense and provided by nature is only available once we combine the theoretical standpoint with the standpoint of a practically grounded metaphysics and its rich notion of the world author as a rational agent aiming at realizing his ultimate end by drawing on the mechanism of nature. Seen from this unified standpoint, this mechanism of nature both feeds in the conditions and provides actions on the part of the human agents regarded as appearances, and these actions ultimately lead to the realization of the end in

---

these very same rational beings which are to turn law (right) into an end of virtue, see Brandt (2013).

[68] This is Paul Guyer's (2011: 116) metaphor.

question. Moreover, this mechanism of nature is at least partially determined by human freedom.

4.3 The Ethical Commonwealth and Perpetual Peace

So far, we have discussed the guarantee thesis with regard only to the objective ultimate end. The strategy is now to show that perpetual peace is a condition for this end and that it therefore inherits this certainty.[69] It is at this point that we encounter a serious difficulty, as Kant's distinction of things in themselves and appearances becomes relevant. After all, the intelligible characters plainly concern the intelligible world of things in themselves and noumena. Simplifying a complex issue significantly, the point which arises is as follows. It is simply not clear why the ultimate objective end needs to be reached by *embodied* creaturely agents, that is, by free agents which form compounds with appearances. Is the second postulate of pure practical reason not a device precisely meant to transfer even the real possibility of the highest good into a transcendent realm? While it is, of course, not immediately clear how one can meaningfully speak of a future development of a 'disembodied' agent qua thing in itself, given the infamous atemporality of this realm, Kant clearly seems to think that this is possible.

Let us assume, however, for the sake of argument, that the end of creation – and I shall keep focusing on its unconditional part, namely, moralization – will indeed certainly come about immanently. This means that the end of creation comes about in the form of the ethical commonwealth,[70] "God's kingdom on earth," as Kant puts it in the *Religion* (6: 93).

The reason, as we can read in the opening passages of the third piece of the *Religion* (6: 93–95), is that without such an ethical commonwealth moral self-perfection is only possible in a limited or negative manner, without removing the danger of a relapse into prioritizing concerns for one's happiness over those regarding morality. A stable good will, the positive variant of moral self-perfection or, as Kant expresses it, the "reign" of "the good principle" (Rel 6: 93) cannot be achieved by embodied free agents in isolation, but in an adequate social context. This social context is the ethical commonwealth.[71]

---

[69] Along these lines, Taylor (2010: 13) maintains that perpetual peace is a necessary condition for each element of the highest good. While I agree that perpetual peace is *conducive* even to the "noumenal ethical community of an afterlife" (Taylor 2010: 22), there clearly seems to be the option of an exclusively transcendent moralization, and it is difficult to see why perpetual peace should be a *necessary* condition for this variant.

[70] For a comprehensive account of Kant's conception of the ethical commonwealth, see Moran (2012).

[71] The indispensability of this social context for moralization has been emphasized by, for example, Wood (1999: 309–320; 2000).

From there we can enquire about the consequences and the presuppositions of this, as we can call it, *world immanent* moralization within the ethical commonwealth. In order to accomplish this, we need to distinguish an imperfect form, that is, something like its "negative surrogate,"[72] and a perfect form of perpetual peace. Put simply and to anticipate, both are necessary conditions of immanent moralization, with the perfect variant of perpetual peace being temporally subsequent and the imperfect version temporally prior to immanent moralization.[73] In the essay *Perpetual Peace* there are indeed indications of both conceptions. In TPP 8: 366 Kant claims that moral improvement or formation ("Bildung") is to be expected within a good legal constitution, albeit with reference to particular states – but as we know, for Kant, a state cannot have a good constitution in isolation. In TPP 8: 378 he maintains in a phrase coined in Biblical terms that perpetual peace is a by-product of the good will. I shall now elucidate this idea of focusing on the presuppositions and consequences of immanent moralization in a bit more detail, starting with a short sketch of what, in Kant's mind, the ethical commonwealth is supposed to look like.

As indicated above, the makeup of the institutional framework of perpetual peace is controversial, since it is unclear whether Kant requires a world republic or a maximally expanded, more or less loose federation for this end. What these two variants have in common is that they are not a first order world state, as a universal monarchy would be. A first order state has human beings as its members. For Kant, the ethical community, while not being a state-like entity in the sense that its laws are noncoercive, does have such a first-order structure. In addition to being a member of the state which is a constitutive member of the legal structure underlying perpetual peace, each human being is, in principle, an immediate member of the ethical commonwealth. Moreover, the ethical community is a cosmopolitan entity, a fusion of particular religions undergoing the process of enlightenment with some regional peculiarities surviving, and as such the truly universal church. The ethical community is thus the flip side of the legal structure sustaining perpetual peace, with this legal structure undergoing significant transformation through the establishment of the ethical community. I cannot discuss the question as to why the ethical community is essentially religious in nature here,[74] but Kant seems to suggest that this is the case.

---

[72] This term has famously been used by Kant in TPP 8: 357 to refer to the constantly expanding federation of states taking the place – perhaps only temporarily – of the world republic.

[73] I am following Molloy (2017: 94), who calls the imperfect version "negative peace," and Kleingeld (2012: 179) here. Whether Kant changed his mind, endorsing the perfect version in his earlier writings and the imperfect version in the later ones, is a different issue. It seems to make better sense to assume that he needed both versions.

[74] See Frierson (2007) as well as Palmquist (2009, 2017). DiCenso (2013) and Molloy (2017) emphasize the importance of religion for politics in Kant in general.

In any event, at this point we can draw on a probably uncontroversial principle, namely, the idea that certainty, understood in the way described above, is closed under entailment, that is, given that p entails q and that p is certain, then, in this case, q is also certain. Clearly, then, the certainty in question gets transferred to both the perfect and the imperfect version of perpetual peace. In other words, provided that we are entitled from a certain perspective – for example, religion or the practical standpoint in general – to claim the future actuality of the objective ultimate end of reason, then the (future) actuality of the necessary conditions of it must also hold.

In this case, we could conclude the investigation, were it not for the objection raised above, namely, that there is the logical possibility of what we could call an Augustinian, transcendent version of a certain future attainment of the end of creation. Along this vein, the spatiotemporal world and the persons acting in it would always be mired in the propensity toward evil and its social ramifications. Moreover, in such a scenario we could no longer claim that perpetual peace, in its imperfect variant, is a precondition of moralization, nor that perpetual peace in its perfect variant is a consequence of a good will situated in a transcendent realm.

Before addressing this objection let us look into the opposite idea of the immanent version of moralization and its implications in a little more detail. Indeed, throughout the pertinent third piece of the *Religion* (6: 93–147) in particular, Kant seems to make rather strong claims, namely, that moralization is something that happens at a certain time in history and is indeed only possible for the agents living at this time in history, because certain conditions need to be in place without which this moralization cannot occur. It is not obvious, though, whether these passages should also be read as a prognosis or merely as a claim about the duty to establish the ethical commonwealth.

The question is then of course: What happens to those unfortunate enough to be born at the wrong time? The second postulate of pure practical reason is perhaps pertinent here insofar as it enables a transcendent moralization as a way out for those who are *dupés* of world history, to modify Kant's provocative phrase in Refl 7059, 19: 238 where he speaks of a "dupé of virtue," however difficult it may be to conceptualize this 'process.' Whether this involves some sort of transcendent community in which such a moralization can occur (corresponding to the earthly ethical community) is something I cannot discuss here. I shall rather focus on moralization as something to occur in human history.

Suffice it to say that the difficulties arising from the apparent restriction of those eligible for a life in the ethical community can possibly be avoided if we assume that Kant intends to keep the two variants of moralization side by side and, to put it rather simply, an immanent and a transcendent version of the highest good along with it. As we shall see, however, for my argument nothing hinges on whether there is both an immanent and a transcendent unconditional aspect of the highest good, let alone whether there is an immanent and a transcendent version of its conditional aspect, although I do think this is in fact Kant's position.

Now, this much is clear: Provided that we can establish that moralization will certainly be reached immanently, presumably side by side with its transcendent variant, we can regress on conditions. Moralization of agents requires the ethical commonwealth and this, in turn, the establishment of an institutional legal setting that sustains perpetual peace, while this institutional setting will itself be transformed in and through an ethical commonwealth.

Let us now address the objection of the exclusive transcendent actualization of the unconditional aspect of the highest good. How can we do this? One way is to try to establish that it is indeed *constitutive* for the end of creation to be realized in an immanent manner. We could argue (i) that there is the duty of establishing or uniting to form the ethical commonwealth, as Kant repeatedly points out in Rel 6: 94–95. Hence, if there is moralization with regard to human beings at all, and there must be moralization as it is the core of the objective ultimate end of creation, such a key duty cannot remain unfulfilled without compromising the overall end. Moreover, we could try to argue in a more metaphysical manner. We could maintain (ii) that Kant must assume that freedom in its perfect form and nature will be united since this ultimate metaphysical challenge cannot fail to be met when, and if, all parties concerned cooperate accordingly. Finally, we could resort to considerations of symmetry: (iii) the inclination toward evil arises in a social context, therefore it will be overcome in a social context.

I think that these arguments are successful in the end, in particular (i), but instead of examining this in more detail I shall rather explore a different line of thought altogether, which is by no means incompatible with the previous line. Strikingly, in a sense we might not need any argument for the *actuality* of immanent moralization to succeed and, in this case, we can in fact leave it open whether they do so. The reason is that the regress on conditions establishing the certainty of perpetual peace may also work on the assumption of the mere, albeit real *possibility* of an immanent actualization of the end of creation in the form of the establishment of an ethical commonwealth. After all, Kant clearly says in Rel 6: 94 that without an underlying legal entity the ethical community cannot be brought about. In addition to this, we can conclude that since the ethical commonwealth is supposed to be truly global in its extension, so must be this very legal entity at its foundation. Hence, this entity must be the one sustaining perpetual peace. Such an emphasis on real possibility would fit perfectly well with the idea that immanent moralization in a social context is an object of hope.[75]

This is Philip Rossi's (2019) point in his Element in this series, although he develops it in a context that is different from the certainty issue with regard to perpetual peace. Rossi reads Kant's critical project in what he calls "anthropological" terms, and hence rejects a narrowly conceived epistemological account. For Rossi, humans are called upon to submit their multifaceted activities in the world to the reigns of reason. This includes the domains of politics and religion, and for Rossi it is important to regard the political and the religious as integral for the highest good possible in the world. Moreover, in Rossi's opinion, the political project of peacemaking needs to be understood as embedded in the larger scheme of attempts to make the highest good actual. As I understand Rossi, a distinction of a perfect and an imperfect version of perpetual peace is endorsed, at least implicitly. Moreover, for Rossi, articulating this vision both in the philosophy of politics and in religion is essential for providing hope and guidance for these very efforts to succeed.

For Kant, at any rate, the actuality of the legal framework sustaining perpetual peace is indeed a necessary condition of the *possibility* of the ethical commonwealth, as the passages from the *Religion* (6: 94) indicate. Provided we can claim that it is *certain* that the ethical commonwealth is (*realiter*) possible in this world, we can draw on our inference pattern and conclude that the actual coming about of perpetual peace (in its imperfect form) as its precondition is certain as well. Clearly, it is fair to maintain the certainty of the real possibility of the ethical commonwealth in this world from a practical point of view since, as we know, for Kant it is a duty of humanity toward itself to establish or unite to form this commonwealth.[76] Moreover, provided that by virtue of it being a duty to establish the ethical commonwealth it is also *certain* that it is a duty to establish the ethical commonwealth, we can draw on the closedness of certainty under entailment. In this vein, the real possibility of the ethical community must also be certain, in which case we can indeed draw on this inference pattern again and conclude that the (future) actuality of perpetual peace is certain. This coheres well with the idea that if there really is a duty of

---

[75] Chignell (2014: 115–117) takes the objects of hope to be characterized by real possibility and emphasizes the status of the ethical commonwealth as being such an object.

[76] Conversely, concerns about 'ought-implies-can' might arise here, since my argument seems to suggest that only those in favorable historical circumstances can have the duty to unite to form a cosmopolitan ethical commonwealth. Kant's point about this duty being addressed to "the entire human race" (Rel 6: 94) rather than to each individual human agent may perhaps mitigate these concerns. This formulation arguably indicates that there must indeed be one point in time at which *all* the human agents *can* unite in this manner, while up to this point everybody needs to do all they can to establish and secure the legal framework for an ethical commonwealth and honor this duty to unite in an indirect manner.

humanity toward itself to unite to form an ethical commonwealth (Rel 6: 95), then, plainly, at least some human agents must be in a position to do so.

Strikingly, this move reconfigures the argument developed so far in a significant manner. The idea had originally been to treat perpetual peace in its imperfect variant as a condition for something which is both the core of the final objective end of creation and a *fulfilled* duty on the part of human agents. Now, however, the focus is on the status of a duty, that is, something normative, namely, the duty to establish the ethical commonwealth regardless of its ultimate fulfillment and regardless of it being achieved as a divine end. In this vein, we have a shift from a practically grounded metaphysical to a moral argument.

Moreover, if there really is a duty to bring about the ethical community in the sense indicated, we can conclude that all the pertinent facets of the problem of freedom can be dealt with since freedom is itself a condition of duty. In particular, we can also conclude that the natural causal facet of the problem of freedom can not only be handled but that the special laws of nature are such that the coming about of perpetual peace is ensured. The question is then about our key sentence in the guarantee footnote (TPP 8: 361.5–8fn) which connects the form of the world to the end of the creator. The answer is that the framework of Kant's practically grounded metaphysics provides some form of explication as to how the congruence of this form of the world of appearances and the duty to bring about the ethical community comes to pass.

We have thus, in fact, identified two possible strategies for arguing for the guarantee thesis in its future actuality reading, with the first drawing on the future actuality, and the second on the real possibility of the immanent form of the unconditional element of the highest good.

5 Concluding Remarks

In this Element, I have tried to answer three questions with regard to Kant's doctrine of a guarantee of perpetual peace which, in my reading, Kant understands in the strong sense of implying a certain 'coming about of it' in the future. I have tried to show that in a specific sense nature and providence are identical, that by virtue of Kant's insistence on the priority of freedom with regard to laws of nature and divine agency, the working of the guarantor powers does not undermine human freedom and the duties grounded on it, and that the guarantee thesis itself is based on a conception of divine knowledge – to be ascribed to the creator of the world taken as a rational agent – about the ultimate compliance with the duty of moral self-perfection on the part of the human free agents. Perpetual peace, the highest political good, is the condition which enables this compliance to materialize in history by making the ethical commonwealth possible. Insofar as the objective ultimate end will come about in history, so will perpetual peace. Arguably, insofar as it is certain that the objective ultimate end *can* come about in history, so also is it certain that there *will* be perpetual peace.

These answers draw on a dimension of Kant's thought which is not usually at the foreground of attention, namely, Kant's practically grounded metaphysics. Kant thinks that by virtue of the validity of moral norms we are committed to a number of claims about transcendent objects, although we can have no knowledge of them. In this downscaled mode, doctrines enter the Kantian universe regarding hypothetical free actions, providence and grace which one would not expect to be there. In this regard, a considerable leaning toward or influence of the Molinist tradition with its emphasis on human freedom and its priority is detectable. If this is indeed the case, the legacy of this tradition of *metaphysical* doctrines extends even further into the history of *legal and political* philosophy than recent scholarship has uncovered.[77]

Still, the reading suggested may, for all the qualifications made, be nonetheless too 'dogmatic' for some readers, especially those who are searching Kant for inspiration to answer pressing questions of contemporary political philosophy and the theory of international relations;[78] the justification of the guarantee thesis in particular may simply look too far removed from these issues.

According to my reading, however, Kant's practically grounded metaphysics is not meant to underpin the normative dimension of his doctrine about peace. On the contrary, for Kant, the dependency holds in the opposite direction. For him, practically grounded metaphysics is, in a sense, a logical extension or something like a consequence of the existence of obligation grounded in autonomy.

Of course, one may not be prepared to follow Kant in this, but a rejection of Kant's conception of a practically grounded metaphysics does not by itself amount to a dismissal of his normative theory of peace. It remains to be seen, however, how the persisting questions about a guarantee of perpetual peace can be answered without endorsing this still unfamiliar side of Kant. Perhaps the only option remaining in this case is reading Kant's claims in a weaker way and maintaining that, for all we can see, nature provides favorable conditions for the highest political good. Kant's own story, or so I believe, is on a much grander scale, though.

---

[77] Piro's (2014) important overview closes with Pufendorf.
[78] See, for example, Hidalgo (2012) and Ion (2012).

Abbreviations

Works by Kant

CPR A/B	*Critique of Pure Reason* 1st and 2nd edition respectively.
CJ	*Critique of the Power of Judgement.*
CF	*The Conflict of the Faculties,* trans. Gregor/Anchor, in Kant (1996b), 233–327.
CPrR	*Critique of Practical Reason,* trans. Gregor, in Kant (1996a), 133–271.
Th-B	*Danzig Rational Theology According to Baumbach,* trans. Fugate/Hymers, in Eberhard and Kant (2016), 131–218.
G	*Groundwork of the Metaphysics of Morals,* trans. Gregor, in Kant (1996a), 37–107.
IUH	*Ideas for a Universal History with a Cosmopolitan Aim,* trans. Wood, in Kant (2007), 107–119.
PhilTh-P	*Lectures on the Philosophical Doctrine of Religion*, trans. Wood, in Kant (1996b), 335–451.
MM	*The Metaphysics of Morals,* trans. Gregor, in Kant (1996a), 353–604.
NE	*A New Elucidation of the First Principles of Metaphysical Cognition,* trans. Walford/Meerbote, in Kant (1992), 1–36.
TPP	*Perpetual Peace: A Philosophical Sketch.*
Refl	*Reflection,* trans. Bowman/Guyer/Rauscher, in Kant (2005).
Rel	*Religion within the Boundaries of Mere Reason*, trans. di Giovanni, in Kant (1996b), 39–215.

Other sources

Concordia	*Liberi arbitrii cum gratiae donis, divina praescientia, providentia, praedestinatione et reprobatione Concordia,* see Molina (1953).
M	*Metaphysica,* see Baumgarten (2013).
STh	*Summa de Theologia,* see Sancti Thomae de Aquino (2000).

Bibliography

With the exception of *the Critique of Pure Reason*, references to Kant's texts are given by indicating the volume and page number of the Akademie-Ausgabe ("AA"), that is, *Immanuel Kant's gesammelte Schriften*. Herausgegeben von der königlich preußischen Akademie der Wissenschaften [und ihren Nachfolgern] (Berlin: Riemer et al. 1900–). With regard to *Perpetual Peace: A Philosophical Sketch*, translations into English are my own from Kant (1796). For an alternative rendering and with regard to references not containing quotations see *Toward Perpetual Peace: A philosophical project*, trans. Mary J. Gregor, in Kant (1996b), 311–351. In all other cases the pertinent volume of *The Cambridge Edition of the Works of Immanuel Kant*, edited by Paul Guyer and Allen W. Wood (Cambridge: Cambridge University Press) has been used.

Ameriks, Karl (2006), *Kant and the Historical Turn: Philosophy as Critical Interpretation* (Oxford: Oxford University Press).

(2012), *Kant's Elliptical Path* (Oxford: Oxford University Press).

Anderson-Gold, Sharon (2012), "The Political Foundations of Prophetic History," in Paul Formosa, Avery Goldman and Tatiana Patrone (eds.), *Politics and Teleology in Kant* (Cardiff: University of Wales Press), 180–193.

Baiasu, Sorin (2018), "Kant's Guarantee for Perpetual Peace: A Reinterpretation and Defence," in Larry Krasnoff, Nuria Sánchez Madrid and Paula Satne (eds.), *Kant's Doctrine of Right in the 21st Century* (Cardiff: University of Wales Press), 181–200.

Baiasu, Sorin, Pihlström, Sami and Williams, Howard (eds.) (2011), *Politics and Metaphysics in Kant* (Cardiff: University of Wales Press).

Baumgarten, Alexander Gottlieb (2013), *Metaphysics. A Critical Translation with Kant's Elucidations, Selected Notes, and Related Materials*. Translated and edited by Courtney D. Fugate and John Hymers (London and New York: Bloomsbury Academic).

Boehm, Omri (2014), *Kant's Critique of Spinoza* (New York: Oxford University Press).

Bouton, Christophe (2007), "Ist die Geschichtsphilosophie eine neue Theodizee?," in Myriam Bienenstock (ed.), *Der Geschichtsbegriff: eine theologische Erfindung?* (Würzburg: Königshausen und Neumann), 69–82.

Brandt, Reinhard (2013), "Ewiger Friede als Natur- und Vernunftzweck," in Stefano Bacin, et al. (eds.), *Kant und die Philosophie in weltbürgerlicher Absicht. Akten des 11. Internationalen Kant-Kongresses, 2010* (Berlin and Boston, MA: De Gruyter), 127–145.

Byrd, B. Sharon and Hruschka, Joachim (2010), *Kant's Doctrine of Right: A Commentary* (Cambridge: Cambridge University Press).

Caranti, Luigi (2012), "The Guarantee of Perpetual Peace: Three Concerns," in Paul Formosa, Avery Goldman and Tatiana Patrone (eds.), *Politics and Teleology in Kant* (Cardiff: University of Wales Press), 145–152.

Chignell, Andrew (2014), "Rational Hope, Possibility, and Divine Action," in Gordon E. Michalson (ed.), *Religion within the Bounds of Mere Reason: A Critical Guide* (Cambridge: Cambridge University Press), 98–117.

(2017), "Knowledge, Discipline, System, Hope: The Fate of Metaphysics in the Doctrine of Method," in James O'Shea (ed.), *Kant's Critique of Pure Reason: A Critical Guide* (Cambridge: Cambridge University Press), 259–279.

Clewis, Robert R. (ed.) (2015), *Reading Kant's Lectures* (Berlin and Boston: De Gruyter).

Craig, William Lane (1987), *The Only Wise God: The Compatibility of Divine Foreknowledge and Human Freedom* (reprinted ed. 2000; Eugene, OR: Wipf and Stock).

Dean, Howard (2012), "Perfected Humanity: Nature's Final End and the End in Itself," in Paul Formosa, Avery Goldman and Tatiana Patrone (eds.), *Politics and Teleology in Kant* (Cardiff: Wales University Press), 228–244.

Dekker, Eef (2000), *Middle Knowledge* (Leuven: Peeters).

Deligiorgi, Katerina (2006), "The Role of the 'Plan of Nature' in Kant's Account of History from a Philosophical Perspective," *British Journal for the History of Philosophy*, 14 (3), 451–468.

(2017), "The Philosopher as Legislator: Kant on History," in Matthew C. Altman (ed.), *The Palgrave Kant Handbook* (London: Palgrave Macmillan), 683–704.

DiCenso, James J. (2013), *Kant, Religion, and Politics* (Cambridge: Cambridge University Press).

Duplá, Leonardo Rodríguez (2016), "Die Kohärenz der Gnadenlehre im kantischen Denken," *Kant-Studien*, 107 (2), 256–290.

Eberhard, Johann Georg and Immanuel Kant (2016), *Preparation for Natural Theology. With Kant's Notes and the Danzig Rational Theology Transcript.* Translated and edited with introduction and notes by Courtney D. Fugate and John Hymers (London and New York: Bloomsbury Academic).

Ertl, Wolfgang (1998), *Kants Auflösung der "dritten Antinomie". Zur Bedeutung des Schöpfungskonzepts für die Freiheitslehre* (Freiburg and Munich: Verlag Karl Alber).

(2004), "Schöpfung und Freiheit. Ein kosmologischer Schlüssel zu Kants Kompatibilismus," in Norbert Fischer (ed.), *Kants Metaphysik und Religionsphilosophie* (Hamburg: Meiner), 43–76.

(2014), "'Ludewig' Molina and Kant's Libertarian Compatibilism," in Matthias Kaufmann and Alexander Aichele (eds.), *A Companion to Luis de Molina* (Boston and Leiden: Brill), 405–445.

(2016), "Die dritte Antinomie und die Unterscheidung von Dingen an sich und Erscheinungen bei Kant," *Nihon Kant Kenkyu*, 18, 66–82.

(2017a), "Home of the Owl? Kantian Reflections on Philosophy at University," *Tetsugaku. International Journal of the Philosophical Association of Japan*, 1, 107–123.

(2017b), "On Christopher Insole's 'Kant and the Creation of Freedom'," *Critique*. https://virtualcritique.wordpress.com/2017/06/28/wolfgang-ertl-on-christopher-insoles-kant-and-the-creation-of-freedom/ (Accessed September 15, 2018).

(2018), "The Guarantee of Perpetual Peace in Kant: Remarks on the Relationship between Providence and Nature," in Violetta L. Waibel, Margit Ruffing and David Wagner (eds.), *Natur und Freiheit. Akten des XII. Internationalen Kant-Kongresses* (IV; Berlin and Boston: De Gruyter), 2539–2548.

Fischer, John Martin (ed.) (1989), *God, Foreknowledge, and Freedom* (Stanford, CA: Stanford University Press).

Flikschuh, Katrin (2006), "Reason and Nature: Kant's Teleological Argument in *Perpetual Peace*," in Graham Bird (ed.), *A Companion to Kant* (Chichester: Blackwell), 383–396.

Flint, Thomas P. (1998), *Divine Providence: The Molinist Account* (Ithaca, NY and London: Cornell University Press).

(2009), "Divine Providence," in Thomas P. Flint and Michael C. Rea (eds.), *The Oxford Handbook of Philosophical Theology* (New York: Oxford University Press), 262–285.

(2011), "Whence and Whither the Molinist Debate: A Reply to Hasker," in Ken Perszyk (ed.), *Molinism: The Contemporary Debate* (New York: Oxford University Press), 37–49.

Förster, Eckhard (2009), "The hidden plan of nature," in Amélie Oksenberg Rorty and James Schmidt (eds.), *Kant's Idea for a Universal History with a Cosmopolitan Aim* (Cambridge, UK: Cambridge University Press), 187–199.

Freddoso, Alfred J. (1988a), "Introduction," in Luis de Molina, *On Divine Foreknowledge: Part IV of the Concordia* (Ithaca, NY and London: Cornell University Press), 1–81.

(1988b), "Medieval Aristotelianism and the Case against Secondary Causation in Nature," in Thomas V. Morris (ed.), *Divine and Human Action. Essays in the Metaphysics of Theism* (Ithaca, NY and London: Cornell University Press), 74–118.

(1991), "God's General Concurrence with Secondary Causes: Why Conservation is not Enough?," *Philosophical Perspectives*, 5, 553–585.

(1994), "God's General Concurrence with Secondary Causes: Pitfalls and Prospects," *American Catholic Philosophical Quarterly*, 67, 131–156.

(2002), "Introduction," in Francisco Suarez, *On Creation, Conservation and Concurrence* (South Bend, IN: St Augustine's Press), xi–cxxiii.

Friedman, Michael (1992), "Metaphysical Foundations of Newtonian Science," in Michael Friedman (ed.), *Kant and the Exact Sciences* (Cambridge, MA and London: Harvard University Press), 136–164.

Frierson, Patrick (2007), "Providence and Divine Mercy in Kant's Ethical Cosmopolitanism," *Faith and Philosophy*, 24 (2), 144–164.

Gerhardt, Volker (1999), *Immanuel Kants Entwurf "Zum ewigen Frieden": Eine Theorie der Politik* (Darmstadt: Wissenschaftliche Buchgesellschaft).

Guyer, Paul (2006), "The Possibility of Perpetual Peace," in Luigi Caranti (ed.), *Perpetual Peace: New Interpretative Essays* (Rome: Luiss University Press), 143–163.

(2011), "Kantian Communities: The Realm of Ends, the Ethical Community, and the Highest Good," in Charlton Payne and Lucas Thorpe (eds.), *Kant and the Concept of Community* (Rochester, NY: University of Rochester Press), 88–120.

Hasker, William (2011), "The (Non-)Existence of Molinist Counterfactuals," in Ken Perszyk (ed.), *Molinism. The Contemporary Debate* (New York: Oxford University Press), 25–36.

Hasker, William, Basinger, David and Dekker, Eef (eds.) (2000), *Middle Knowledge: Theory and Applications* (Frankfurt/M: Peter Lang).

Hegel, Georg Friedrich Wilhelm (2010), *The Science of Logic*. Translated by George di Giovanni (Cambridge: Cambridge University Press).

Hidalgo, Oliver (2012), *Kants Friedensschrift und der Theorienstreit in den internationalen Beziehungen* (Wiesbaden: Verlag für Sozialwissenschaften).

Hoesch, Matthias (2014), *Vernunft und Vorsehung: Säkularisierte Eschatologie in Kants Religions- und Geschichtsphilosophie* (Berlin and Boston: De Gruyter).

Höffe, Otfried (2004), "Weltrepublik oder Völkerbund?," in Otfried Höffe (ed.), *Immanuel Kant: Zum ewigen Frieden* (Berlin: Akademie-Verlag), 77–93.

Hogan, Desmond (2014), "Kant on Foreknowledge of Contingent Truths," *Res Philosophica*, 91 (1), 47–70.

(forthcoming), "Kant's Theory of Divine and Secondary Causation," in Brandon Look (ed.), *Leibniz and Kant* (New York: Oxford University Press).

Hübener, W (1989), "Praedeterminatio physica," in Joachim Ritter and Karlfried Gründer (eds.), *Historisches Wörterbuch der Philosophie* (7; Basel: Schwabe), 1216–1225.

Insole, Christopher J. (2015), *Kant and the Creation of Freedom: A Theological Problem* (Oxford: Oxford University Press).

Ion, Dora (2012), *Kant and International Relations Theory: Cosmopolitan Community-building* (London and New York: Routledge).

Kant, Immanuel (1796), *Zum ewigen Frieden: Ein philosophischer Entwurf.* Neue vermehrte Auflage (Königsberg: Nicolovius).

(1992), *Theoretical Philosophy, 1755–1770.* Translated and edited by David Walford in collaboration with Ralf Meerbote (Cambridge: Cambridge University Press).

(1996a), *Practical Philosophy.* Translated and edited by Mary J. Gregor. General Introduction by Allen Wood (Cambridge: Cambridge University Press).

(1996b), *Religion and Natural Theology.* Translated and edited by Allen W. Wood and George di Giovanni (Cambridge: Cambridge University Press).

(1998), *Critique of Pure Reason.* Translated by Paul Guyer and Allen W. Wood (Cambridge: Cambridge University Press).

(2001), *Critique of the Power of Judgement.* Edited by Paul Guyer, translated by Paul Guyer and Eric Matthews (Cambridge: Cambridge University Press).

(2005), *Notes and Fragments.* Edited by Paul Guyer, translated by Curtis Bowman, Paul Guyer and Frederick Rauscher (Cambridge: Cambridge University Press).

(2007), *Anthropology, History, and Education.* Edited by Robert B. Louden and Günter Zöller, translated by Mary J. Gregor et al. (Cambridge: Cambridge University Press).

Kaufmann, Matthias and Aichele, Alexander (2014), *A Companion to Luis de Molina* (Boston, MA and Leiden: Brill).

Kleingeld, Pauline (2001), "Nature or Providence? On the Theoretical and Moral Importance of Kant's Philosophy of History," *American Catholic Philosophical Quarterly*, 75 (2), 201–219.

(2004), "Approaching Perpetual Peace: Kant's Defence of a League of States and His Ideal of a World Federation," *European Journal of Philosophy*, 12, 304–325.

(2012), *Kant and Cosmopolitanism: The Philosophical Ideal of World Citizenship* (Cambridge: Cambridge University Press).

Lehner, Ulrich (2007), *Kants Vorsehungskonzept auf dem Hintergrund der deutschen Schulphilosophie und -theologie* (Leiden: Brill).

Lloyd, Genevieve (2009), "Providence as Progress: Kant's variations on a tale of origins," in Amélie Oksenberg Rorty and James Schmidt (eds.), *Kant's Idea for a Universal History with a Cosmopolitan Aim: A Critical Guide* (Cambridge: Cambridge University Press), 200–215.

Loux, Michael J. (2006), *Metaphysics: A Contemporary Introduction*, 3rd ed. (London and New York: Routledge).

Ludwig, Bernd (2005), "Zum Frieden verurteilt? Was 'garantiert' die Natur in Kants Traktat vom Ewigen Frieden?," *Jahrbuch für Recht und Ethik*, 13, 275–286.

(2015), "'Die *Kritik der reinen Vernunft* hat die Wirklichkeit der Freiheit nicht bewiesen, ja nicht einmal deren Möglichkeit': Über die folgenreiche Fehlinterpretation eines Absatzes in der Kritik der reinen Vernunft," *Kant-Studien* (106), 398–417.

MacGregor, Kirk R. (2015), *Luis de Molina: Life and Theology of the Founder of Middle Knowledge* (Grand Rapids, MI: Zondervan).

Mackie, John L. (1974), *The Cement of the Universe: A study of causation* (Oxford: Clarendon).

McCarty, Richard (2009), *Kant's Theory of Action* (New York: Oxford University Press).

Mertens, Thomas (1995), "Zweckmäßigkeit der Natur und politische Philosophie bei Kant," *Zeitschrift für philosophische Forschung*, 49 (2): 220–240.

Molina, Ludovici (1953), *Liberi arbitrii cum gratiae donis, divina praescientia, providentia, praedestinatione et reprobatione Concordia*. Ed. crit. cur. Iohannes Rabeneck S.I. (Oniae, Matriti).

Molina, Luis de (1988): *On Divine Foreknowledge: Part IV of the Concordia*. Translated, with an introduction and notes, by Alfred J. Freddoso. (Ithaca, NY and London: Cornell University Press)

Molloy, Seán (2017), *Kant's International Relations: The Political Theology of Perpetual Peace* (Ann Arbor, MI: University of Michigan Press).

Moore, Jennifer (1992), "Kant's ethical community," *The Journal of Value Inquiry*, 26 (1), 51–71.

Moran, Kate A. (2012), *Community and Progress in Kant's Moral Philosophy* (Washington, DC: Catholic University of America Press).

Muchnik, Pablo and Pasternack, Lawrence (2017), "A Guide to Kant's Treatment of Grace," *Con-Textos Kantianos*, 6. https://www.con-textoskantianos.net /index.php/revista/article/ view/292 (Accessed September 15, 2018).

Palmquist, Stephen R. (2009), "Kant's Religious Argument for the Existence of God: The Ultimate Dependence of Human Destiny on Divine Assistance," *Faith and Philosophy*, 26 (1), 3–22.

(2017), "Kant's Model for Building the True Church: Transcending 'Might Makes Right' and 'Should Makes Good' through the Idea of a Non-Coercive Theocracy," *Diametros*, 54, 76–94.

Pasternack, Lawrence (2014), *Routledge Philosophy Guidebook to Kant on Religion within the Boundaries of Mere Reason* (London and New York: Routledge).

(2017), "Restoring Kant's Conception of the Highest Good," *Journal of the History of Philosophy*, 55 (3), 435–468.

Pereboom, Derk (2006), "Kant on Transcendental Freedom," *Philosophy and Phenomenological Research*, LXXIII (3), 537–567.

Perszyk, Ken (2011a), "Introduction," in Ken Perszyk (ed.), *Molinism: The Contemproary Debate* (New York: Oxford University Press), 1–25.

Perszyk, Ken (ed.) (2011b), *Molinism: The Contemporary Debate* (New York: Oxford University Press).

Piro, Francesco (2014), "The Philosophical Impact of Molinism in the 17th Century," in Matthias Kaufmann and Alexander Aichele (eds.), *A Companion to Luis de Molina* (Leiden and Boston: Brill), 365–403.

Pogge, Thomas (2009), "Kant's Vision of a Just World Order," in Thomas E. Hill Jr. (ed.), *The Blackwell Guide to Kant's Ethics* (Chichester: Wiley-Blackwell), 196–208.

Reath, Andrews (1988), "Two Conceptions of the Highest Good in Kant," *Journal of the History of Philosophy*, 26 (4), 593–619.

Rosefeldt, Tobias (2012), "Kants Kompatibilismus," in Andree Hahmann, Mario Brandhorst and Bernd Ludwig (eds.), *Sind wir Bürger zweier Welten? Freiheit und moralische Verantwortung im transzendentalen Idealismus* (Hamburg: Meiner), 77–109.

Rossi, Philip J. (2019), *The Ethical Commonwealth in History* (Cambridge: Cambridge University Press).

Sancti Thomae de Aquino (2000), Opera omnia recognovit ac instruxit Enrique Alarcón automato electronico Pampilonae ad Universitatis Studiorum Navarrensis aedes. http://www.corpusthomisticum.org/iopera.html/ (Accessed October 30, 2018).

Silber, John R. (1959), "Kant's Conception of the Highest Good as Immanent and Transcendent," *Philosophical Review*, 68 (4), 469–492.

Taylor, Robert S. (2010), "Kant's Political Religion: The Transparency of Perpetual Peace and the Highest Good," *The Review of Politics*, 72 (1), 1–24.

Trinkaus Zagzebski, Linda (1991), *The Dilemma of Freedom and Foreknowledge* (New York and Oxford: Oxford University Press).

van Inwagen, Peter (1983), *An Essay on Free Will* (Oxford: Oxford University Press).

Vilhauer, Benjamin (2004), "Can We Interpret Kant as a Compatibilist about Determinism and Moral Responsibility?," *British Journal for the History of Philosophy*, 12 (4), 719–730.

Watkins, Eric (2005), *Kant and the Metaphysics of Causality* (Cambridge: Cambridge University Press).

(2014b), "What is, for Kant, a Law of Nature?," *Kant-Studien*, 105 (4), 471–490.

(2017), "Kant on the Unity and Diversity of Laws," in Michela Massimi and Angela Breitenbach (eds.), *Kant and the Laws of Nature* (Cambridge: Cambridge University Press), 11–29.

Wierenga, Edward (2011), "Tilting at Molinism," in Ken Perszyk (ed.), *Molinism: The Contemporary Debate* (New York: Oxford University Press), 118–139.

Willaschek, Marcus (1992), *Praktische Vernunft: Handlungstheorie und Moralbegründung bei Kant* (Stuttgart and Weimar: Metzler).

(2016), "Must We Believe in the Realizability of Our Ends? On a Premise of Kant's Argument for the Postulates of Pure Practical Reason," in Thomas Höwing (ed.), *The Highest Good in Kant's Philosophy* (Berlin and Boston: De Gruyter), 223–244.

Williams, Howard (1996), *International Relations and the Limits of Political Theory* (Basingstoke: Palgrave Macmillan).

(2011), "Metaphysical and not just Political," in Sorin Baiasu, Sami Pihlström and Howard Williams (eds.), *Politics and Metaphysics in Kant* (Cardiff: University of Wales Press), 215–232.

Wood, Allen W. (1984), "Kant's Compatibilism," in Allen W. Wood (ed.), *Self and Nature in Kant's Philosophy* (Ithaca, NY and London: Cornell University Press), 73–101.

(1999), *Kant's Ethical Thought* (Cambridge: Cambridge University Press).

(2000), "Religion, Ethical Community and the Struggle against Evil," *Faith and Philosophy*, 17 (4), 498–511.

(2005), *Kant* (Malden, MA: Blackwell).

(2006), "Kant's Philosophy of History," in Pauline Kleingeld (ed.), *Immanuel Kant: Toward Perpetual Peace and Other Writings on Politics, Peace, and History*, translated by David. L. Colclasure (New Haven and London: Yale University Press), 243–262.

Yovel, Yirmiahu (1980), *Kant and the Philosophy of History* (Princeton, NJ: Princeton University Press).

Ypi, Lea (2010), "Natura daedala rerum? On the Justification of Historical Progress in Kant's *Guarantee of Perpetual Peace*," *Kantian Review*, 14 (2), 118–148.

Zöller, Günter (2016), " 'The Supersensible . . . in Us, above Us and after Us': The Critical Conception of the Highest Good in Kant's Practico-Dogmatic Metaphysics," in Thomas Höwing (ed.), *The Highest Good in Kant's Philosophy* (Berlin and Boston: De Gruyter), 263–280.

Acknowledgments

I should like to thank audiences in Frankfurt, Mainz, San Diego, St Andrews and Vienna for very helpful comments on papers related to the topic of this Element and, in particular, Marcus Willaschek, Eric Watkins and Jens Timmermann. Karl Ameriks' notes on the entire final draft have been an extremely precious gift for which I am deeply grateful. Thanks are also due to the participants of my graduate seminar on *Perpetual Peace* at Keio University, Tokyo in 2017–18, to the two referees and to Howard Williams for their most helpful suggestions and also to Yuka Takedomi, Ian Platt and Kayoko Nohara. Work on this Element has been generously supported by a *kakenhi* grant from the Japan Society for the Promotion of Science.

Cambridge Elements ⹀

The Philosophy of Immanuel Kant

Desmond Hogan
Princeton University
Desmond Hogan joined the philosophy department at Princeton in 2004. His interests include Kant, Leibniz and German rationalism, early modern philosophy, and questions about causation and freedom. Recent work includes 'Kant on Foreknowledge of Contingent Truths', *Res Philosophica* 91 (1) (2014); 'Kant's Theory of Divine and Secondary Causation', in Brandon Look (ed.), *Leibniz and Kant*, Oxford University Press (forthcoming); 'Kant and the Character of Mathematical Inference', in Carl Posy and Ofra Rechter (eds.), *Kant's Philosophy of Mathematics Vol. I*, Cambridge University Press (2019).

Howard Williams
University of Cardiff
Howard Williams was appointed Honorary Distinguished Professor at the Department of Politics and International Relations, University of Cardiff in 2014. He is also Emeritus Professor in Political Theory at the Department of International Politics, Aberystwyth University, a member of the Coleg Cymraeg Cenedlaethol (Welsh-language national college) and a Fellow of the Learned Society of Wales. He is the author of *Marx* (1980); *Kant's Political Philosophy* (1983); *Concepts of Ideology* (1988); *International Relations in Political Theory* (1992); *Hegel, Heraclitus and Marx's Dialectic; International Relations and the Limits of Political Theory* (1996); *Kant's Critique of Hobbes: Sovereignty and Cosmopolitanism* (2003), *Kant and the End of War* (2012) and is currently editor of the journal *Kantian Review*. He is writing a book on the Kantian legacy in political philosophy for a new series edited by Paul Guyer.

Allen Wood
Indiana University
Allen Wood is Ward W. and Pricilla B. Woods Professor at Stanford University. He was a John S. Guggenheim Fellow at the Free University in Berlin, a national Endowment for the Humanities Fellow at the University of Bonn and Isaiah Berlin Visiting Professor at the University of Oxford. He is on the editorial board of eight philosophy journals, five book series and the *Stanford Encyclopedia of Philosophy*. Along with Paul Guyer, Professor Wood is co-editor of the Cambridge Edition of the *Works of Immanuel Kant* and translator of the *Critique of Pure Reason*. He is the author or editor of a number of other works, mainly on Kant, Hegel and Karl Marx. His most recently published book, *Fichte's Ethical Thought*, was published by Oxford University Press in 2016. Wood is a member of the American Academy of Arts and Sciences.

About the series

This Cambridge Elements series provides an extensive overview of Kant's philosophy and its impact upon philosophy and philosophers. Distinguished Kant specialists will provide an up–to–date summary of the results of current research in their fields and give their own take on what they believe are the most significant debates influencing research, drawing original conclusions.

Cambridge Elements $\equiv$

The Philosophy of Immanuel Kant

Elements in the Series

Formulas of the Moral Law
Allen Wood

The Sublime
Melissa McBay Merritt

Kant's Power of Imagination
Rolf-Peter Horstmann

Kant on Civil Society and Welfare
Sarah Holtman

The Ethical Commonwealth in History: Peace-Making as the Moral Vocation of Humanity
Philip J. Rossi

Kant on the Rationality of Morality
Paul Guyer

The Guarantee of Perpetual Peace
Wolfgang Ertl

A full series listing is available at: www.cambridge.org/EPIK

Printed in the United States
By Bookmasters